The Next Visitor
to Planet Earth

Other books by Michael Esses:
Michael, Michael, Why Do You Hate Me?
The Phenomenon of Obedience
Jesus in Genesis

The Next Visitor
to Planet Earth

by the Reverend Michael Esses, D.H.L.
edited by Irene Burk Harrell

Logos International
Plainfield, New Jersey

Acknowledgments

Scripture quotations herein are from *The Amplified Bible (The Amplified Old Testament* is copyright © 1962, 1964 by the Zondervan Publishing House, used by permission, *The Amplified New Testament* is copyright © 1958 by the Lockman Foundation, used by permission).

To My Children—Kathleen, John, and
Laurie—who have shown me that
the path to heaven is the "faith of a child"

Contents

Editor's Foreword

There is an ever-growing expectancy among believers that we will see the Lord in our day. It is only natural that we should be curious about the whens and wherefores of such eagerly awaited events as Jesus' Second Coming, the Rapture of the Saints, and the Millennium in which Christ will reign on earth for a thousand years. That we can't know everything in no way diminishes our desire to know as much as possible. And the Scriptures do not disappoint us. They provide much food for thought in many prophetic utterances—in the Old Testament and the New—about the events before, during, and after the great and glorious day when Jesus will fulfill His own promise, "Behold, I come quickly."

Many of the Scriptures regarding the end times are hidden from our eyes, however, until someone points them out and illumines them with what God has revealed about them. One modern-day Bible teacher who is well-equipped to open these Scriptures for us is completed Jew, Mike Esses, for whom the Holy Scriptures are as alive and full of meaning as is the Living Word, Jesus Himself, who stood in Mike's room one night and called him by name, changing the entire course of his life in a single moment. In these pages, the author of the powerful *Michael, Michael, Why Do You Hate Me?* shares some of the insights God has given him about the events of the end times.

The privilege of editing Dr. Esses' spoken messages for book publication in this and two preceding volumes has been a real joy to me, an important avenue for God's blessing in my life. It is my prayer that God will bless you with a fuller appreciation of His incomparably wonderful Word as you read, and that your heart will be made ready to receive with great joy, *The Next Visitor to Planet Earth.*

Irene Burk Harrell

Preface

How I delight in the wonder that I, a Jew, can write about the Second Coming of my Messiah. It is still a source of never-ending amazement to me that Jesus reached down and revealed Himself to me from amongst my brethren.

Prophets from the beginning of time have written about the Day of the Lord, and now in our day and age we are seeing their prophecies come to pass.

How many have been fulfilled and how many are yet to be fulfilled? In the lectures from which the manuscript for this book was prepared, I've tried to answer these questions and others that are prevailing among God's people.

Everywhere I speak, everywhere I teach, no matter where I am on the face of this earth, the queries are still the same: When is He coming? How long do we have to get ready?

The lesson is always the same: The time is not important. The salient point is *Be ready.* Be ready with your heart swept clean. Be ready with your oil lamps full. Be ready with your mind fixed on the mind of God—for your Redeemer draweth nigh!

The Next Visitor
to Planet Earth

Part I

The Last Days

Chapter 1

Signs of the End Times

"Behold, I come quickly," Jesus promises us in the last chapter of the Bible. And everywhere, believers pray, "Amen. Even so, come, Lord Jesus."

Indeed, the Second Coming of Jesus has been eagerly anticipated by Christians ever since the first disciples saw Him ascend into heaven (Acts 1:9-11). Jesus had just finished telling His disciples to go back and wait in Jerusalem until they had been baptized with the Holy Ghost. They would, He said, receive power—miracle-working power—and they would be His witnesses to the uttermost parts of the earth.

When he had told them these things, He was lifted up from their midst, and a cloud, a sign of the presence of the Living God, took Him out of their sight. As they stood staring after Him, two men in white—a couple of angels—suddenly appeared among them and said,

> *Men of Galilee, why do you stand gazing into heaven? This same Jesus, Who was caught away and lifted up from among you into heaven, will return in just the same way in which you saw Him go into heaven. (Acts 1:11)*

The angels said *that* Jesus would come back, and *how* He would return, but they didn't say *when* it would happen. And ever since that day, men have looked up into the clouds and wondered, "When will it be? Will it be today?"

Throughout history, Christians have had many different opinions about these questions, but no one has known the answer for certain. Jesus Himself had told the disciples earlier, when they had asked Him when the end would be and when He would come back,

> *Of that exact day and hour, no one knows, not even the angels of heaven, nor the Son, but only the Father. (Matt. 24:36)*

Nevertheless, some have been so sure they had figured out the exact time of His return that they have dressed in white and gathered on hillsides, looking up into the sky until their necks were stiff, their feet tired, their hearts discouraged, but they haven't seen Him come.

Jesus warned that this would be so, that men would say, "Look, here is Christ," or "There He is," but they would all be impostors. "When I come back," Jesus told them, "you won't need anyone to make an announcement about it, for all men will know. My coming will not be hidden":

> *For just as the lightning flashes from the east and shines and is seen as far as the west, so will the coming of the Son of man be. (Matt. 24:27)*

We will know when He has come. In the meantime, He gave us many signs that would be fulfilled before His arrival. And He said that the generation that saw the fulfillment of all of the signs would not pass away before His return. I believe this generation is our own!

Many of the signs Jesus gave us are front-page headlines in today's newspapers. The end times *are* with us. Very soon, we can expect to look up and see our Savior returning in clouds of glory, just as He said He would, and exactly according to His timetable.

The prophet Hosea says a very strange and interesting thing about the timetable of the Second Coming of Jesus:

> *Come, and let us return to the Lord; for He has so torn that He may heal us; He has stricken so that He may bind us up. After two days He will revive us—quicken us, give us life; on the third day, He will raise us up, that we may live before Him. (Hos. 6:1-2)*

The psalmist said that a day with the Lord is as a thousand years, and so there is a sense in which Jesus has been gone only two days instead of two thousand years. We're in the twilight of that second day, and God's Word, speaking through the prophet Hosea, tells us that on the third day, He will raise us up that we may live before Him. The third day, which is dawning upon us, will be the thousand years when Jesus will reign on earth, the years of the Millennium. "He has torn that He may heal; He has stricken that He may bind," means that He is preparing His Body of believers. The Bridegroom is coming back for His bride, to revive us, to quicken us, to give us life—everlasting life with Him.

Let us look at some of the signs Jesus gave the disciples of the end times that are being fulfilled before our eyes as the second day draws to a close:

> *Jesus answered them, Be careful that no one misleads you, for many will come in My name, saying, I am the Messiah, the Christ; and they will lead many astray. (Matt. 24:4-5)*

> *And many false prophets will rise up and deceive and lead many into error. (Matt. 24:11)*

Many such impostors have already come. Today there is a teenager who flies around in his own 747 airplane. He has thousands of followers, millions of dollars at his disposal. Many people are hailing this Guru as the Savior, as the Christ, and he is leading the people astray.

We can tell a false preacher, a false prophet, from a real preacher, a true prophet of God, because the Lord has given us His Holy Spirit, and one of the gifts of the Spirit is that of the discernment of spirits. The minute somebody stands up before you and departs from the Word of God, giving you his own false interpretation, you should be able to feel it like an alarm bell going off inside you. A false prophet will be speaking about I, I, me, me. He will say, "Look to me. I have done this and that."

> *And you will hear of wars and rumors of wars; see that you are not frightened or troubled, for this must take place, but the end is not yet. (Matt. 24:6)*

In the last hundred years, we have had more wars on the face of the earth, more rumors of wars, than in all the time since the beginning of time. But there's no way we can have peace until the King of peace comes back.

> *Nation will rise against nation, and kingdom against kingdom, and there will be famines and earthquakes in place after place. (Matt. 24:7)*

This is happening with us now, and it has been happening continually in the last hundred years. Nation has been rising against nation, kingdom against kingdom. Famine is widespread. In India today, ten thousand people will die of starvation. Ten thousand more will die tomorrow. And in the last hundred years, we have had more earthquakes than in any comparable period since the creation of the earth. All these signs are with us now. Jesus gave them to us that we might recognize the end times and be prepared for them.

> *And this good news of the kingdom, the Gospel, will be preached throughout the whole world as a testimony to all the nations, and then will come the end. (Matt. 24:14)*

We have not had the means of preaching the Gospel to all nations in the past, but we have it now—satellites, video tapes, audio tapes, translations of the Scriptures into many languages never before written down. Everyone is having a chance to hear the Gospel. The Bible does not say that all nations will accept the Good News, but all will have a chance to hear it.

> *And there will be signs in the sun, the moon, the stars, and upon the earth distress of nations . . . and men's hearts failing them for fear. (Luke 21:25-26)*

Men's hearts *are* failing them for fear. The world is going crazy trying to figure out what's happening to the monetary system. Everyone who doesn't know Jesus is running scared in every nation on the face of the earth. World leaders are standing in fearful expectation—they know something is about to happen, and they are frightened because they don't know that the Lord Jesus is on His way back. And all these things are but the beginning of sorrows, Jesus said (Matt. 24:8). Things will get so bad that

> *If those days had not been shortened, no human being would endure and survive; but for the sake of the elect, God's chosen ones, those days will be shortened. (Matt. 24:22)*

In addition to recording Jesus' own statements about the signs of the end times, the writers of the New Testament spoke of a number of other signs as well:

> *In the last days, there will set in perilous times of great stress and trouble. (II Tim. 3:1)*

These are perilous times because we have the power to blow ourselves off the face of the earth, and we don't know what nut is going to push what button somewhere and end the whole thing. The newspapers are full of reports of the perilous times in which we are living as the signs of the end times are taking place.

> *People will be lovers of self and utterly self-centered, lovers of money and aroused by an inordinate desire for wealth, proud and arrogant and contemptuous boasters. They will be abusive, disobedient to parents, ungrateful, unholy and profane. (II Tim. 3:2)*

Anyone with eyes and ears knows that these things are going on all around us. The prophecy about disobedience to parents doesn't refer only to teenagers, but to those in our generation as well. As our parents are living longer, we are disobedient, failing to honor them as the Lord commanded us in His Word. Instead of taking them into our own homes and lovingly caring for them, we stick them in old folks' homes. We're too busy—we can't be bothered. They're a lot of trouble, and we are too selfish, too disobedient, to put up with them.

The one commandment that carries a promise with it is the one that directs us to honor our father and our mother that our days may be prolonged upon the face of the earth. If you want to live to a ripe old age, you should honor your father and your mother. The Lord says, "If you refuse to honor your earthly father and mother, how can you possibly honor, revere, and respect Me, your heavenly Father? If you put your parents in an old folks' home, maybe you will put Me in an old folks' home when you think I am too old for you, too worn out, so you can no longer hear My voice."

> *In the end times, men will be lovers of pleasure rather than lovers of God. For although they hold a form of piety, a form of religion, they deny the power of it. (II Tim. 3:4b-5)*

In the end times, men will have a form of godliness but they will deny the power of God. They will stand up in the pulpit. They will preach the Gospel. They will give altar calls and invitations. People will come forward. They will be baptized. They will be saved, but yet, the preacher will deny the power of God. There will be no place on the program for the power of God to heal anybody, to deliver anybody, to fill anybody with the Holy Ghost, because the minister will deny there is such a thing as the power of God to do anything.

Jesus said there would come a day when men would come before Him and say, "Lord, Lord, I've traveled all over the world for You. I've ministered for You. I've preached in Your name. I've baptized in Your name." And Jesus will say, "Get away from Me, you worker of iniquity, for I know you not. You made a profession with your lips, but you did not really believe with your heart. You denied My power. You gave me lip service, but the attitude of your heart was never right. I honored My word, not you, when the people came to hear you, because I will never fail My people. I brought forth miracles for them because they believed Me. They made a profession with their lips, and with their heart they were right with Me. But you are a hypocrite for calling upon Me and yet denying My power."

> *Wicked men and impostors will go on from bad to worse, deceiving and leading astray others and being deceived and led astray themselves. (II Tim. 3:13)*

There will be two groups of people in the end times—the Body of believers whom Christ is calling to Himself from all over the face of the earth, and those who will stand in their own arrogance and get worse and worse. Everywhere we look, we see two spirits being poured out in the last days. One is the Holy Spirit of God being poured out on all flesh, just as God promised through the prophet Joel. Peter quoted him when he said,

> *And it shall come to pass in the last days, saith God, I will pour out My Spirit upon all flesh, and your sons and your daughters shall*

prophesy, and your young men shall see visions, and your old men shall dream dreams. (Acts 2:17-18)

The other spirit being outpoured is the spirit of the enemy, Satan. Anyone with the gift of discernment will know which spirit is of Satan and which is of God. Today, the spirit of the enemy is manifesting himself among men who have rejected God. We find churches for homosexuals, churches of Satan offering up human sacrifices, men going from the vile to the more vile.

Jesus warned that in the end times, it would be as it was in the days of Noah (Matt. 24:27), when there was immorality, sexual perversion, drunkenness, disobedience to parents. And we do have all these abominations with us today as well as some that men never dreamed of in the days of Noah—a flood of filth and pornography on the newsstands, in the moving-picture theaters, and even coming over the TV set into your living room.

> *In latter times, some will turn away from the faith, giving attention to deluding and seducing spirits and doctrines that demons teach. (I Tim. 4:1)*

> *The time is coming when people will not tolerate sound and wholesome instruction, but . . . they will gather to themselves one teacher after another . . . chosen to satisfy their own liking and to foster the errors they hold. They will turn aside from hearing the truth and wander off into myths and man-made fictions. (II Tim. 4:3-4)*

As Christ prepares His Body of believers, as He prepares His Bride without spot or blemish or wrinkle, there will be others who will fall away from the faith. It's happening today, just as Paul prophesied in his letters to Timothy.

As people fall away from the faith, they will not want to hear the sound doctrine of Jesus Christ, Him crucified, dead, buried, and resurrected. They will want to hear about everything else—but not about Jesus. They will be scoffers who will have nothing to do with the Second Coming of Jesus.

> *Scoffers, mockers, will come in the last days with scoffing; people who walk after their own fleshly desires, saying, Where is the promise of His coming? For since the forefathers fell asleep, all things have continued as they did from the beginning of creation. . . . Nevertheless, do not let this fact escape you, beloved, that with the Lord, one day is as a thousand years, and a thousand years as one day. The Lord does not delay and be tardy or slow about what He promises . . . but He is long-suffering, extraordinarily patient, toward you, not desiring that any should perish, but that all should turn to repentance. (II Pet. 3:3b-4, 8-9)*

"We've got plenty of time yet to do our own thing," these scoffers boast. "We've heard this story for the last two thousand years, that Christ is coming soon, but we don't believe it. We don't want to hear any more about it. He wasn't really here in the first place, and He's not coming again. It's just make-believe. Let us eat, drink, and be merry because tomorrow, when we're six feet under, that's all there is. We can't take it with us, because we're not really going anywhere, so why not live it up while we can?"

These scoffers are going to be in for a rude awakening when they go through the door of death and find themselves standing there all alone. But when I go through that door, I know that my Jesus will be there waiting for me. And He will take me in and present me to the Father, saying, "This is Mike. He is one of Mine."

In the Book of Daniel, the prophet said that in the end times,

> *. . . many shall run to and fro. (Dan. 12:4b)*

In the Hebrew, that means they're going to be running around like chickens with their heads cut off. Men are not going to know what they're doing. They hold peace conferences, not at a quiet retreat in some secluded area of the world where they can really commune with God and seek His will, but they meet in Paris, the sin capital of the world.

Knowledge shall be increased and become great. (Dan. 12:4c)

Knowledge has increased in the last 150 years more than in all the preceding years since the beginning of time. God has given man the ability to destroy himself if he wants to. He has also given him the ability to be totally and completely healed of every affliction. He has a chance to stand up and say, "I will be counted with the people of God," or "I will stay in my intellect. I am a self-made man. Because of my own great wisdom, skill, and knowledge, I discovered this particular vaccine all by myself. God had nothing to do with it."

So they say, ignorant of the fact that all knowledge comes from God, and all authority stems from the Lord.

Another sign of the end times that God has given through the Old Testament prophets is that the Jews would be returning to Palestine:

> *And now therefore thus says the Lord, the God of Israel, concerning this city of which you say, It shall be delivered into the hand of the king of Babylon by sword and by famine and by pestilence: Behold I will gather them out of all countries to which I drove them in My anger and in My wrath and in great indignation; I will bring them again to this place, and I will make them dwell safely; And they shall be My people, and I will be their God. (Jer. 32:36-38)*

Jews *are* returning to Palestine today, in great numbers.

And we have already seen the fulfillment of a promise the Lord gave to Isaiah:

> *Who has heard such a thing? Who has seen such things? Shall a land be born in one day, or shall a nation be brought forth in a moment? For as soon as Zion was in labor, she brought forth her children. (Isa. 66:8)*

No one had ever heard of a nation being born in a single day, because never in the history of the world had such a thing happened before. But Israel became a recognized nation, actually born in one day.

After being away from their homeland for almost two thousand years, the Jews were emboldened to begin settling again in Palestine by the Balfour declaration of November, 1917. In 1922, the League of Nations gave Great Britain the mandate over Palestine. As recommended by a special committee of the United Nations, the state of Israel was established by decree of May 15, 1948 in the partition of Palestine between Jews and Arabs.

Jude wrote,

> *In the last days, in the end times, there will be scoffers who seek to gratify their own unholy desires, following after their own ungodly passions. (Jude 18)*

The unholy desires spoken of here are not limited to the things that are usually thought of as lusts of the flesh. They also embrace desire for material possessions and lust for world power. A struggle for world power is taking place right now, a worldwide conspiracy that is beyond our imagination.

The coming of a world dictator is clearly prophesied in the Scriptures:

> *But relative to the coming of our Lord Jesus Christ, the Messiah, and our gathering together to meet Him, we beg you, brethren, not to allow your minds to be quickly unsettled or disturbed or kept excited or alarmed, whether it be by some pretended revelation of the Spirit or by word or by letter alleged to be from us, to the effect that the day of the Lord has already arrived and is here. Let no one deceive or beguile you in any way, for that day will not come except the apostasy comes first, that is, unless the predicted great falling away of those who have professed to be Christians has come, and the man of lawlessness is revealed, who is the son of doom, who opposes and exalts himself so proudly and insolently against all that is called God or that is worshiped, even to his actually taking his seat in the temple of God, proclaiming that he himself is God. (II Thess. 2:1-4)*

> *As I stood on the sandy beach, I saw a beast coming up out of the sea with ten horns and seven heads. . . . And to him the dragon gave his own might and power, and his own throne and great dominion. And . . . the whole earth went after the beast in amazement and admiration. They fell down and did homage to the dragon, because he had bestowed on the beast all his dominion and authority; they also praised and worshipped the beast . . . and he was given freedom to exert his authority and to exercise his will during forty-two months (three and half years). And he opened his mouth to speak slanders against God, blaspheming His name and His abode, even vilifying those who live in heaven. He was further permitted to wage war on God's holy people and to overcome them. And power was given him to extend his authority over every tribe and people and tongue and nation, and all the inhabitants of the earth will fall down in adoration and pay him homage, every one whose name had not been recorded from the foundation of the world in the Book of Life of the Lamb. (Rev. 13:1-8)*

The Lord told us that the world dictator, the beast, would be coming up out of the sea, and He gave us other clues about him in Revelation 13. The beast will have the power of speech, and he will use it to speak slanderous things against God, blaspheming God. He will be permitted to wage war against God's holy people, His saints, and to overcome them. All the inhabitants of the earth will bow down in adoration to pay him homage—everyone whose name has not been recorded from the foundation of the world in the Lamb's Book of Life.

There is a second beast with all the rights and powers of the first one spoken of in the same chapter of Revelation. He will rise up out of the land:

> *Then I saw another beast rising up out of the land; he had two horns like a lamb, and he spoke (roared) like a dragon. (Rev. 13:11)*

Look at one of the things the second beast will do:

> *He compels all alike, both small and great, both the rich and the poor, both free and slave to be marked with an inscription stamped on their right hands or on their foreheads. So that no one will have power to buy or sell unless he bears the stamp, mark, or inscription, that is, the name of the beast or the number of his name. (Rev. 13:16-17)*

This beast will do away with the present monetary system, putting us on a worldwide credit system. There is already in the works, a plan to take us off all existing currencies and put us on a one-world computer.

When you go to some department stores today to buy something, the clerk punches a number into a computer, and almost instantly, the machine tells her whether your credit is all right or not. This system will be working all over the world when we go off the present monetary system.

There will come a day when you will be required to have this number stamped on your forehead or on your hand with ink visible only under a special light. Yet if we permit the mark of the beast to be imprinted upon our hand or forehead, we will be doomed. Believers will have to make a choice. We will have to stand together as a Body of believers if we are here during the time of the Tribulation.

> *Whoever pays homage to the beast and his statue and permits the beast's stamp to be put on his forehead or on his hand, he too shall have to drink of the wine of God's indignation and wrath . . . and he shall be tormented with fire and brimstone in the presence of the Holy angels and in the presence of the Lamb. And the smoke of their torment ascends forever and ever, and they have no respite day or night. (Rev. 14:9b-11a)*

I believe this coming world dictator prophesied in the Book of Revelation is with us today. We don't know who he is, but in time he will be revealed. And the Lord has told us the numerical value of the name of the world dictator:

> *Here is room for discernment—a call for the wisdom of interpretation; let any one who has intelligence, penetration, and insight enough, calculate the number of the beast, for it is a human number—the number of a certain man; his number is six hundred and sixty-six. (Rev. 13:18)*

There are new steam buses in Los Angeles and in San Francisco with the serial number 666 on top. I have seen shoes coming in from Italy with the trademark of the European Common Market on them. It is a circle with a line drawn through the middle of it with the number 666 on the bottom and the picture of a lamb on top with horns, exactly as described in the Book of Revelation.

And we are seeing that number all over Jerusalem these days. Every vehicle in the public transportation system has the number 666 on it. It's on trucks, buses, and taxicabs.

There's an air of anxiety all over the Middle East, not only with the Jews, but with the Arabs, with all people. They're expecting some great miracle to take place. Rabbis who today are expecting the Messiah to come very soon have referred to the twelfth chapter of Daniel to work out the mathematics of His coming.

> *And from the time that the continual burnt offering is taken away, and the abomination that makes desolate is set up, there shall be a thousand two hundred and ninety days. Blessed, happy, fortunate, spiritually prosperous and to be envied is he who waits expectantly and earnestly—who endures without wavering beyond the period of tribulation—and comes to the thousand three hundred and thirty-five days. (Dan. 12:11-12)*

The rabbis insist that "days" means "years" and have taken the two figures, 1290 and 1335, added them together, and come up with the year 2625. Subtracting from that 721, the year when the northern kingdom of Israel was destroyed by the kingdom of Assyria, they get 1904, a very important year. In 1904, there was a great outpouring of the Holy Spirit in Wales, and in 1906, at Azusa Street in Los Angeles.

The burnt offering was taken away in A.D. 70, when Titus came into Jerusalem and destroyed the temple. The rabbis added the year 70 to 1904 and decided the Messiah would be coming in 1974. But 1974 turned into 1975, and they're still looking. That's all right. No man can know exactly when. That's God's business.

In the end times, we will see that this world dictator will give Israel the very thing that she thinks she wants the most—worldwide credit to buy arms, munitions, Phantom jets, things they don't have enough of now. And Israel will worship him. They will hail him as the Messiah. But the Scripture tells us that after three and a half years, he will walk into the temple that will have been rebuilt* and will say, "Worship me." And the people of Israel will know that once again they have picked a loser. They will know he is the Antichrist, Mr. 666, and not the Messiah.

---

* See *Logos Journal* news item reprinted on page 00

Chapter 2

Get Ready for the Rapture!

The end times are closing in. The Day of the Lord is near:

> But as to the suitable times and the precise seasons and dates, breth-
> ren, you have no necessity for anything being written to you. For you
> yourselves know perfectly well that the day of the Lord's return will
> come as unexpectedly and suddenly as a thief in the night. When
> people are saying, All is well and secure, and There is peace and
> safety, then in a moment, unforeseen destruction will come upon
> them as suddenly as labor pains come upon a woman with child;
> and they shall by no means escape, for there will be no escape. (I
> Thess. 5:1-3)

In the end times, we will have world leaders telling us
that we will have peace and safety in our time. I remember
Chamberlain coming back from Munich saying, "I believe it is
peace for our time . . . peace with honor." Less than twelve
months later, the Second World War erupted. We thought it
was the last war, but a few short years later, we were engaged
in a "police action" in Korea in which thousands were killed.
No matter how much men cry, "Peace and safety," we're not

going to see peace and safety until the King of peace Himself comes back, until Jesus Christ returns and reigns.

His coming could be any day now. In James 5:8, we read that the coming of the Lord draweth nigh. In Matthew 24:44, Jesus tells us to be ready, for in such an hour as we think not, at the time we least expect it, the Son of man will come. Most of us act as if we have much time left. But many of the signs of the end times have already been fulfilled. We should be ready, with our sandals on our feet, our knapsacks on our backs, just as the people of Israel were told to do in the exodus from Egypt. He tells us the same thing, because He is coming back in the twinkling of an eye.

> *For the Lord Himself will descend from heaven with a loud cry of summons, with the shout of an archangel, and with the blast of the trumpet of God. And those who have departed this life in Christ will rise first. Then we, the still living who remain [on the earth], shall simultaneously be caught up along with the resurrected dead in the clouds to meet the Lord in the air; and so always—through the eternity of the eternities—we shall be with the Lord! (I Thess. 4:16-17)*

There are three theories about what Christians call the Rapture of the Church, the taking up of the Body of believers to meet Jesus in the air. One says that when the Bridegroom comes for His bride, the Body of believers will be taken up right away. The second says that we will have to spend the first three and half years of the tribulation, the times of troubles, on earth, and then we will be taken up. A third says that all believers will have to go through the entire tribulation before they are taken up. And each can be backed up by Scripture. We won't know who is right until the time comes. Then we will know.

We think we have been seeing a great move of the Holy Spirit in our day, but we haven't begun to see Him moving in the way that He will move very soon now. It is time to get our hearts ready, to prepare ourselves for the Second Coming of Christ.

After giving us many signs of His Second Coming, Jesus warned us:

> *Watch you, therefore, and pray always that you may be accounted worthy to escape all these things that shall come to pass, and to stand before the Son of man. (Luke 21:36)*

There is a way of escape. God has provided it for us in Jesus:

> *For God so loved the world that He gave His only begotten Son that whosoever believes in Him should not perish, but have everlasting life. (John 3:16)*

Romans 10:9 says that if you profess with your lips that Jesus is Lord and believe with your heart that God raised Him from the dead, you shall be saved. Jesus is the way of escape, the only way. The world as we know it will come to an end, but we will not perish with it; we will have everlasting life if we have Jesus.

> *Except you repent, you shall all likewise perish. (Luke 13:5)*

The Lord is expecting the obedience of His people in these end times, and to be obedient, we must repent. Christ has already taken our sins and iniquities from us, but we have to turn from our wicked ways and say, "Lord, I admit I am a sinner. Have mercy on me. I accept the sacrifice of Jesus Christ and I repent of my sin." When we do that, He does forgive.

When a man knows that God has forgiven him, Satan will try to bring to his mind the sins of the past. But the Lord forgets all about our sin once we have confessed it to Him. And we are to forgive ourselves, and to forget our sins, not

keep on dredging them up time after time. We need to say,
"This is the day that the Lord has made. It is a new day. I shall
rejoice and be glad in it. I am a new creature because my sins
are forgiven." Once we have been cleansed from all unrighteousness, we can look for Jesus' Second Coming with eager
anticipation, and not with fear.

Some men have made the wrong kind of preparation for
the last days. James wrote about them:

> *You have heaped together treasure for the last days. . . . But your
> abundant wealth has rotted . . . and your gold and silver are com-
> pletely rusted through. (James 5:3b, 2-3a)*

Those men who think they can get ready for the end
times by piling up material possessions are in for a rude awakening.

The Holy Spirit, speaking through the apostle Paul, gave
us some special instructions about how to get ready:

> *Furthermore, brethren, we beg and admonish you in virtue of our
> union with the Lord Jesus, that you follow the instructions which
> you learned from us about how you ought to walk so as to please
> and gratify God, as indeed you are doing; that you do so even more
> and more abundantly—attaining yet greater perfection in living
> this life. For you know what charges and precepts we gave you on
> the authority and the inspiration of the Lord Jesus. (I Thess.
> 4:1-2)*

The risen Christ met Paul on the road to Damascus when
Paul was on his way to persecute the church. Paul believed he
was doing God's work—until the risen Christ met him and
said, "Paul, why do you persecute Me?" Later Paul was taken
by the Lord into the Arabian Desert where the Lord transformed that mind of the Pharisee of the tribe of Benjamin
into the mind of Paul the Apostle.

Jesus is still in the business of changing lives and transforming minds and hearts. Paul had to be changed to see

people through the eyes of Jesus Christ. The Lord wants all of us to see our fellowman through His eyes. Paul's calling, his authority, his inspiration were given to him by the Lord Jesus Himself.

> *For this is the will of God, that you should be consecrated—separated and set apart for pure and holy living: that you should abstain and shrink from all sexual vice. (I Thess. 4:3)*

In Paul's day, the early Christians had natural tendency to turn back to the sexual vice that prevailed in the area at the time. And Paul admonished the Thessalonians to abstain from these evil practices.

> *Each one of you should know how to possess, control, manage, his own body in purity, separated from things profane, and in consecration and honor. (I Thess. 4:4)*

When you separate yourself, you are honoring the Lord Jesus Christ. He says that you are

> *not to be used in the passion of lust, like the heathen who are ignorant of the true God and have no knowledge of His will. (I Thess. 4:5)*

You know God's will is that you are to be separate, that you are to be in the world, but not part of it. And you have to fight the world, the flesh, and the devil. We fight the world by staying in Jesus Christ. We fight our flesh by dying to our flesh daily. And we fight the devil by using the sword of the Spirit, the Word of God. And we will always win the fight when we recognize that Jesus has already defeated the enemy on the cross.

Paul, giving us further counsel about the last days, says,

> *Let no man transgress, and overreach his brother and defraud him in this matter or defraud his brother in business. For the Lord is an*

> *avenger in all these things, as we have already warned you sol-*
> *emnly and told you plainly. (I Thess. 4:6)*

The Lord is the avenger if you defraud your brother.
The Lord will not stand for it. He requires us to deal with one
another in love.

> *For God has not called us to impurity, but to consecration, to dedi-*
> *cate ourselves to the most thorough purity. (I Thess. 4:7)*

We are to be consecrated to Him as His bride.

> *Therefore whoever disregards and sets aside and rejects this disre-*
> *gards not man but God, Whose very Spirit Whom He gives to you*
> *is holy, chaste, pure. But concerning brotherly love for all other*
> *Christians, you have no need to have any one write you, for you*
> *yourselves have been personally taught of God to love one another.*
> *(I Thess. 4:8-9)*

In Jesus' story of the Good Samaritan, a man was lying by
the wayside, hurt. A priest passed by him and didn't do a
thing to help. And then came a Levite, a lower priest, and he
didn't do anything either. The priest and the Levite refused
because helping the injured man would have meant they
would have become ceremonially unclean, and they would
have had to go outside the camp for seven days and seven
nights, separating themselves from the body of believers.
They would miss the offering of the tithe that would be coming to them, so it would cost them a buck. And then they
would have to go and be immersed in water once again. It was
just too much trouble to help out somebody who was hurt.

Then there came along a half-Jew, a Samaritan, who
helped his brother.

And Jesus said, "This is the thing you ought to do. Two
commandments I give you, reducing all the Ten Commandments, all of the 613 rabbinical laws to only two—I'm giving

them to you wholesale: Love the Lord your God with all your heart, soul and mind, and love your neighbor as yourself."

How do you love the Lord with all your heart? His law is inscribed upon the heart of flesh He gives you when you receive Him. His law was not inscribed upon the old stony heart you were born with. We are to look at our neighbors and at everybody else in the same way God looks at us. How does Jesus look at you and me? He looks beyond the green dress, the pink shirt, and the wrinkled tie, and He sees your real needs. Then He supplies those needs in terms of the end product He is planning for your life.

How do you love Him with all your soul? The soul is the will, the intellect, and the emotions. And He says, "Can you will to say, 'Jesus, I love You. I will praise You in all circumstances, in all things'?"

And He says, "If you're an intellectual, will you love Him by faith? Can you get emotional about Jesus and care less if people call you a charismaniac?" A charisma is a gift from God that releases us so that we are able to worship Him in spirit and in truth, with a song of praise and thanksgiving. And it makes no difference what denomination we come from. We can worship Him together as one Body of believers.

You can get emotional about the Lord. There's nothing wrong with it. We see King David rejoicing before the ark of the covenant, dancing in the square before the ark as he brought it into Jerusalem. As he danced, his wife stuck her head out the window, disgusted.

"You're making a mockery of yourself, King David. The king of Israel showing his britches. What kind of a king are you already yet?"

The Lord dealt with her, because she didn't come against David, she came against the Holy Spirit.

Before the Lord dealt with me in my life, I used to get up in the morning and look in the mirror. There I saw the most perfect human being anybody ever saw. And I used to rationalize and excuse myself for everything, because I was absolutely perfect until the Lord said, "You're not such a hot-shot." And He started transforming my life.

"You see the way you excuse yourself?" He said. "That's the way I want you to love that creep next door that you can't stand. Excuse him like you excuse yourself. Love him, like you love yourself."

> *And indeed you are already extending and displaying your love to all the brethren through Macedonia. But we beseech and earnestly exhort you, brethren, that you excel in this matter more and more. To make it your ambition and definitely endeavor to live quietly and peacefully, to mind your own affairs and to work with your hands, as we charged you. (I Thess. 4:10-11)*

If you're not working with your hands, your tongue will start to work. And the tongue can kill. Once it has said something, it can't ever take it back.

> *So that you may bear yourselves becomingly, be correct and honorable and command the respect of the outside world, being self-supporting, dependent on nobody and having need of nothing. (I Thess. 4:12)*

When the world of unbelievers sees you and me living a respectable life, they're going to say, "Gee, there's something different about that person. He lives quietly, he's peaceful, he minds his own business, he never judges, he never criticizes, never grumbles about anything. He's busy all the time. He always has a smile on his face. And no matter what happens, he always says, 'Praise the Lord.' He's got something, and I want it." And when their curiosity gets the best of them, and they ask you why you are like you are, you can tell them about Jesus.

We are to depend on and have need of the Lord Jesus Christ—and nothing else. He has come into the world to give us life and to give it to us more abundantly. All we need to do is reach up our hand and touch the hem of His garment and appropriate the promises He has given us—all seventy-seven hundred promises in the Bible. They're all ours, and we can take them by faith.

> *Now also we would not have you ignorant, brethren, about those who fall asleep in death, that you may not grieve for them, as the rest do who have no hope beyond the grave. (I Thess. 4:13)*

We have hope, don't we? When my little three-and-a-half-year-old boy died in a fire,* Betty and I knew beyond a shadow of a doubt that he was with the Lord Jesus Christ. To be absent from the body is to be with the Lord. Among Donnie's first words were "Jesus," and "Praise the Lord." And we know that we'll see him again.

We do have hope beyond the grave. We're only upon the face of this earth a short time. If we live to be seventy or eighty years of age, we think we've attained to a ripe old age. But what about all eternity? If we're saved, we are with the Lord. We have the hope of seeing Him, and all our loved ones who knew Him, beyond that door which is called death.

> *For since we believe that Jesus died and rose again, even so God will also bring with Him through Jesus those who have fallen a-sleep in death. For this we declare to you by the Lord's own word, that we who are alive and remain until the coming of the Lord, shall in no way precede into His presence or have any advantage at all over those who have previously fallen asleep in Him in death. For the Lord Himself will descend from heaven with a loud cry of summons, with the shout of the archangel, and with the blast of the trumpet of God. And those who have departed this life in Christ will rise first. Then we who are still living who remain on the earth, shall simultaneously be caught up along with the resur-rected dead in the clouds to meet the Lord in the air. And so al-ways, through the eternity of the eternities, we shall be with the*

---

*See account in *Michael, Michael, Why Do You Hate Me?* (Plainfield, N.J.: Logos International, 1973)

Lord! Therefore, comfort and encourage one another with these words. (I Thess. 4:14-18)

The day of resurrection is almost upon us. So the Lord says through His Holy Spirit to you and me that we should be ready, that we should be prepared, that our lives should be pure, consecrated to the Lord Jesus Christ. We are not to be like those foolish virgins, ten of them, five of them waiting and ready, the other five waiting but without oil in their lamps. While they were gone to the store to buy oil for their lamps, the Bridegroom came, and they missed the whole thing. You and I have to be filled to the brim with the Lord Jesus Christ in a life of purity, consecrated to Him, so we won't miss the bridegroom.

Part II

Zechariah Gets It All Together

Chapter 3

Zechariah 1-6

We know very little about the prophet Zechariah except that he was the son of Berechiah and the grandson of Iddo. Iddo was of the priestly tribe, a high priest among the exiles who returned with Zerubbabel from the captivity in 536 B.C. Zechariah himself was considered a rebel because he had not adhered rigidly to the past. He chose to move by the Spirit of God, so his utterances are important to Jews and Christians. Let us see what he had to say:

> *In the eighth month, in the second year of the reign of Darius, came the word of the Lord to Zechariah—(Zech. 1:1a)*

The Word of the Lord, Jesus Christ Himself, the Logos, appeared personally to Zechariah. In the beginning was the Word, and the Word was with God, and the Word was God, and the same Word appeared to Zechariah;

> *the son of Berechiah, the son of Iddo, the prophet, saying, The Lord was very angry with your fathers. Therefore say to them, the Jews of this day, Thus says the Lord of hosts: Return to Me, says the Lord of hosts, and I will return to you. It is the utterance of the*

31

> *Lord of hosts. Be not as your fathers, to whom the former prophets*
> *cried, Thus says the Lord of hosts: Return now from your evil ways*
> *and your evil doings; but they would not hear or listen to Me, says*
> *the Lord. (Zech. 1:1b-4)*

Zechariah's ancestors had been in a constant state of disobedience against the Lord. He sent them prophet after
prophet, but they didn't listen. In that day, if they didn't like
the message of the prophet, they couldn't go to another
church where they could hear something they liked better.
So, when they didn't like the message of the prophet, they
killed him. That's what happened to Zechariah in the end. He
was brought into the temple of the Lord, where he was killed
before the Ark of the Covenant. The Israelites didn't like his
message of a coming day when a Messiah would stand on the
Mount of Olives, when a Savior would come and redeem Israel.

The Lord asked the people of Israel, through the
prophet Zechariah,

> *Your fathers, where are they? And the prophets, do they live*
> *forever? (Zech. 1:5)*

"At first, your fathers didn't listen to me," God said.
"Where are they now? And did any of the messengers I sent
to you have everlasting life?"

> *But My words and My statutes, which I commanded My servants*
> *the prophets, did they not overtake and take hold of your fathers?*
> *(Zech. 1:6a)*

"Were your fathers taken hold of and brought under
conviction by the living Word of God? Or were their hearts so
hardened that they couldn't feel a thing? Did they have hearts
of stone, or did they have hearts of flesh?"

> *So they repented and said, As the Lord of hosts planned and pur-*

posed to do to us, according to our ways and according to our do-
ings, so He has dealt with us. (Zech. 1:6b)

The people did repent, they acknowledged that they had
sinned. "What we are receiving is just what we deserve," they
said.

Upon the twenty-fourth day of the eleventh month, which is the
month of Shebat, in the second year of the reign of Darius, again
the word of the Lord came to Zechariah, the son of Berechiah, the
son of Iddo, the prophet.

Zechariah said, I saw in the night a vision, and behold a man
riding upon a red horse, and he stood among the myrtle trees that
were in a low valley or bottom, and behind him there were horses,
red, bay, or flame-colored, and white. Then I said, O my lord,
what are these?

And the angel who talked with me said, I will show you what
these are. And the man who stood among the myrtle trees answered
and said, These are they whom the Lord has sent to walk to and fro
through the earth and patrol it.

And the men on the horses answered the Angel of the Lord
who stood among the myrtle trees, and said, We have walked to
and fro through the earth, patrolling it, and behold, all the earth
sits at rest, in peaceful security.

Then the Angel of the Lord said, O Lord of hosts, how long
will You not have mercy and loving-kindness for Jerusalem and
the cities of Judah, against which You have had righteous indigna-
tion these seventy years of the Babylonian captivity?

And the Lord answered the angel that talked with me with
gracious and comforting words. So the angel who talked with me
said to me, Cry out, Thus says the Lord of hosts: I am jealous—
righteously indignant—with a great righteous indignation. And I
am very angry with the nations that are at ease; for while I was but
a little displeased, they helped forward the affliction and disaster.
Therefore, thus says the Lord: I have returned to Jerusalem with
compassion, loving-kindness, and mercies. My house shall be built
in it, says the Lord of hosts, and a measuring line shall be stretched
out over Jerusalem with a view to rebuilding its walls. Cry yet
again, saying, Thus says the Lord of hosts: My cities shall yet
again overflow with prosperity, and the Lord shall yet comfort
Zion and shall yet choose Jerusalem.

> *Then I lifted up my eyes, and saw, and behold four horns, which are symbols of strength. And I said to the angel who talked with me, What are these?*
>
> *And he answered me, These are the horns, these are the powers, which have scattered Judah, Israel, and Jerusalem. (Zech. 1:7-19)*

Today's European Common Market approximately encompasses the old Roman Empire. And the four great powers who destroyed Israel were Assyria, Babylon, the Medo-Persian Empire, and the Roman Empire.

Zechariah said,

> *Then the Lord showed me four smiths or workmen, one for each enemy horn, to beat it down. Then said I, What are these horns and smiths coming to do?*
>
> *And he said, These are the horns or powers that scattered Judah, so that no man lifted up his head. But these smiths or workmen have come to terrorize them and cause them to be panic-stricken, to cast out the horns or powers of the nations who lifted up their horn against the land of Judah to scatter it.*
>
> *And I lifted up my eyes and saw, and behold, a man with a measuring line in his hand. Then said I, Where are you going?*
>
> *And he said to me, To measure Jerusalem, to see what is its breadth and what is its length.*
>
> *And behold, the angel who talked with me went forth, and another angel went out to meet him, and he said to the second angel, Run, speak to this young man, saying, Jerusalem shall be inhabited and dwell as villages without walls, because of the multitude of people and livestock in it. (Zech. 1:20-21; 2:1-4)*

This prophecy says that in the end times, Jerusalem will be without walls, a city at peace. This has not yet come to pass. Jerusalem still has walls. At Jesus' Second Coming, Jerusalem will not need walls,

> *For I, says the Lord, will be to her a wall of fire round about, and I will be the glory in the midst of her (Zech. 2:5)*

Jesus will be Jerusalem's shield, and the Holy Spirit will be the glory in the midst of Jerusalem.

> *Ho! Ho! Hear and flee from the land of the north, says the Lord, and from the four winds of the heavens, for to them have I scattered you, says the Lord. (Zech. 2:6)*

There are still over three million Jews in the north, in Russia. But the Lord says that in the end times, the Jews are to flee from the land of the north, to get out of Russia and return to Israel from the four winds of the heavens where He has scattered them. Nobody will have the power to stop them, because the Lord has spoken, and it shall come to pass. Then the Lord said,

> *Ho! Escape to Zion, you who dwell with the daughter of Babylon! (Zech. 2:7)*

The spirit of Babylon is the spirit of the anti-Christ. And that spirit is very powerful in Russia, but the Word of the Lord comes forth out of Zion.

> *For thus said the Lord of hosts, after His glory had sent me, His messenger, to the nations who plundered you, for he who touches you touches the apple or the pupil of His eye. (Zech. 2:8)*

This is complete, divine protection: Any man who touches you is touching the pupil of the Lord's eye. The Lord is saying, "I'm very sensitive in that area of My divine protection. Nobody will be able to stop you when I say, 'Escape to Zion,' because I have prepared the escape for you."

> *Behold, I will swing my hand over them, and they shall become plunder for those who served them. Then you shall recognize and know that the Lord of hosts has sent me, His messenger. Sing and rejoice, O daughter of Zion; for, lo, I come, and I will dwell in the midst of you, says the Lord. (Zech. 2:9-10)*

The Lord of hosts will come and be the *shekinah* glory, the Holy Spirit, in the midst of His people. We are the temple of the living God, the temple of the Holy Spirit. "I will dwell in the midst of you," says the Lord.

> *And many nations shall join themselves to the Lord in that day, and shall be My people. (Zech. 2:11a)*

The people of Israel couldn't accept the message that God had chosen many other people besides those of Israel. How dare the Lord choose a bunch of Gentiles!

> *And I will dwell in the midst of you, and you shall know, recognize, and understand that the Lord of hosts has sent me, His messenger, to you. And the Lord shall inherit Judah as His portion in the holy land, and shall again choose Jerusalem. (Zech. 2:11b-12)*

The Lord Himself will inherit the land of Judah. When Judah was born, the Holy Spirit descended upon Leah, and the words came forth from her mouth, saying, "This time I will praise the Lord." She said that because Jesus Christ would come from the tribe of Judah. Once again the Lord will choose Jerusalem.

> *Be still, all flesh, before the Lord, for He is aroused and risen from His holy habitation. (Zech. 2:13)*

This verse is speaking of the coming Messiah. All flesh will recognize Jesus Christ as the Savior of the world as He gets up from His holy habitation in heaven and comes back to earth again.

> *Then the guiding angel showed me Joshua the high priest standing before the Angel of the Lord, and Satan standing at Joshua's right hand to be his adversary and to accuse him. (Zech. 3:1)*

The scene has shifted for the third vision. In the first vision, Zechariah saw the horses, then he had the vision of the end times when God will choose Jerusalem. Now, Zechariah has been transported by God's Holy Spirit to heaven. And he sees Joshua and Satan standing before the Angel of the Lord.

> *And the Lord said to Satan, The Lord rebuke you, O Satan. Even the Lord Who now habitually chooses Jerusalem, rebuke you! Is not this returned captive Joshua a brand plucked out of the fire? (Zech. 3:2)*

In Jude 9, when the archangel Michael was contending with Satan for the body of Moses, he didn't use his own authority and power to rebuke Satan, but he said, "The Lord rebuke you." The power that overcomes evil is only in the Lord Jesus.

> *Now Joshua was clothed with filthy garments, and was standing before the Angel of the Lord. (Zech. 3:3)*

Why was Joshua, a high priest, wearing filthy garments as he stood before Jesus? Because our righteousness before Christ is as filthy rags.

Jesus is the greatest garbage collector in the world. He went into the world in the flesh. He was tempted on all points like we are. We pray, saying, "Deliver us from evil," but we permit ourselves to be led into temptation. So when we turn back to Christ and ask forgiveness, He takes our sins away. He is just and faithful to forgive us our sin and to cleanse us from all unrighteousness.

> *And He spoke to those who stood before him, saying, Take away the filthy garments from him. And He said to Joshua, Behold, I have caused your iniquity to pass from you, and I will clothe you with rich apparel. (Zech. 3:4)*

The Angel of the Lord removed from Joshua all his sin and iniquity, just as Jesus removed it from you and me.

And I, Zechariah, said, Let them put a clean turban upon his head. So they put a clean turban on his head, and they clothed him with rich garments. And the Angel of the Lord–Jesus Christ Himself–stood by. And the Angel of the Lord solemnly and earnestly protested and affirmed to Joshua, saying, Thus says the Lord of hosts: If you will walk in My ways, and keep My charge, then also you shall rule My house and have charge of My courts, and I will give you access to My presence and places to walk among those who stand here. (Zech. 3:5-7)

The Lord says, "*If* you are obedient, *if* you will walk in My ways of righteousness, *if* you will keep My charge to love the Lord your God with all your heart, soul, and mind, and to love your neighbor as yourself, you will have access to My presence, My Holy Spirit, My dynamite from on High. This is the greatest gift I could possibly give any human being, and I will give it to you, *if—*"

We have two covenants—the big *IF* covenant, and the big *BUT* covenant. The Lord says to us, "If you will walk in My ways—" and we say to the Lord, "*But* Lord, I can't do it."

It's true, we can't do a thing by ourselves. The Lord understands that, however, and He has made full provision for our helplessness. "It's not by might, not by will power, but by My Spirit," says the Lord, "that you can be changed into the kind of people who are pleasing to Me. You will never move and arrive anywhere without My Spirit. If you don't have My Spirit, you're going to be standing still. And the only way you're going to receive My Spirit," says the Lord, "is *if* you'll walk in My ways, *if* you'll keep My charge."

"But Lord, I can't do anything right. I'll never make it."

"That's right. On your own, you're a goner. That's why I sent My Son, Jesus. He will not merely *show* you the way. He will *be* the way for you. All you have to do is receive Him." Jesus said, "I go to prepare a place for you." The place is in heaven, among those who stand with the saints.

Hear now, O Joshua the high priest, you and your colleagues who usually sit before you; for they are men who are a sign or omen, types of what is to come; for behold, I will bring forth My servant the Branch. (Zech. 3:8)

The Branch is Jesus Christ.

For behold, upon the stone which I have set before Joshua, upon that one stone are seven eyes, or facets, the all-embracing providence of God and the sevenfold radiations of the Spirit of God. (Zech. 3:9)

Revelation 1:4 speaks of the same sevenfold Holy Spirit, and Isaiah, prophesying about the coming of Jesus, described the sevenfold nature of the Holy Spirit that would rest upon Him:

And the Spirit of the Lord shall rest upon Him, the spirit of (1) wisdom and (2) understanding, the spirit of (3) counsel and (4) might, the spirit of (5) knowledge and of the (6) reverential and (7) obedient fear of the Lord. (Isa. 11:2)

Behold, I will carve upon it its inscription, says the Lord of hosts, and I will remove the iniquity and the guilt of this land in a single day. And in that day, says the Lord of hosts, you shall invite each man his neighbor under his own vine and his own fig tree. (Zech. 3:9b-10)

Inviting your neighbor to come sit under your vine, under your own fig tree, would be a fulfillment of Leviticus 19:18, which says, "You shall not take revenge or bear any grudge against the sons of your people, but you shall love your neighbor as yourself." Jesus said that was the second great commandment, and it will be fullfilled at the time of His Second Coming.

The angel who talked with me came again, and awakened me, like a man who is awakened out of his sleep. And he said to me, What do you see? I said, I see, and behold, a lampstand all of gold, with

> *its bowl for oil on the top of it, and its seven lamps on it. There are seven pipes to each of the seven lamps which are upon the top of it. (Zech. 4:1-2)*

This Scripture is related to Revelation 1:20 which tells us that the seven lampstands are the seven churches.

> *And there are two olive trees by it, one upon the right side of the bowl, and the other upon the left side of it, feeding it continuously with oil. (Zech. 4:3)*

What do these two olive trees stand for? According to the Revelation to John, they are witnesses:

> *These witnesses are the two olive trees and the two lampstands which stand before the Lord of the earth. And if anyone attempts to injure them, fire pours from their mouth and consumes their enemies. If anyone should attempt to harm them, thus he is doomed to be slain. (Rev. 11:4-5)*

Almost every Bible scholar has his own theory as to who these witnesses are. Some say they are Moses and Enoch. Some say they are Elijah and Enoch. Some say they are Moses and Elijah. Some say they are the archangels Michael and Gabriel. But nobody *knows* who they are. The secret things of God belong to God, and He's not about to reveal them to us right now.

> *The secret things belong unto the Lord our God; but the things which are revealed belong to us and to our children for ever, that we may do all of the words of this law. (Deut. 29:29)*

Whoever they are, these two witnesses have supernatural power. Fire pours from their mouths to consume their enemies. And they have even more power than that! Listen:

> *These two witnesses have the power to shut up the sky, so that no*

> *rain may fall during the days of their prophesying, their prediction of events relating to Christ's kingdom and its speedy triumph. And they also have the power to to turn the waters into blood, to smite and scourge the earth with all manner of plagues, as often as they choose. But when they have finished their testimony and their evidence is all in, the beast, the monster that comes up out of the abyss, out of the bottomless pit, will wage war on them and conquer them and kill them. (Rev. 11:6-7)*

For a time, the witnesses have power to shut up the sky, to turn water into blood, but after the testimony of the two witnesses is in, after their prophecy is finished, their mission on earth is finished. Then they lose their power, and the enemy, the anti-Christ, can come against them and kill them.

> *And their dead bodies will lie exposed in the open street, in a public square, of the great city which is in a spiritual sense called by the mystical and allegorical names of Sodom and Egypt, where also their Lord was crucified. For three and a half days men from the races and tribes and languages and nations will gaze at their dead bodies and will not allow them to be put in a tomb. And those who dwell on the earth will gloat and exult over them and rejoice exceedingly, taking their ease and sending presents in congratulation to one another, because these two prophets had been such a vexation and trouble and torment to all the dwellers on the face of the earth. (Rev. 11:8-10)*

What had happened to the Body of believers in the meantime? They had gone up to be with the Lord. The Rapture had taken place, and we were having a marriage supper with the Lamb that was slain.

> *But after three and a half days, by God's gift the breath of life again entered into them, and they rose up on their feet and great dread and terror fell on those who watched them. Then the two witnesses heard a strong voice from heaven calling to them, Come up here! And before the very eyes of their enemies they ascended into heaven in a cloud. (Rev. 11:11-12)*

*So I asked the angel who talked with me, What are these, my lord?
Then the angel who talked with me answered me, Do you not know
what these are? And I said, No, my lord. Then he said to me, This
addition of the bowl to the candlestick, causing it to yield a cease-
less supply of oil from the olive trees, is the word of the Lord to
Zerubbabel, saying, Not by might, nor by power, but my My Spirit
of Whom the oil is a symbol, says the Lord of hosts. (Zech. 4:4-6)*

The Lord will not move by might, nor by power, but by
His Holy Spirit. No nation will be able to succeed by might.
No person will be able to move in power except those who are
in the Spirit of the Lord, the Holy Spirit of God.

*For who are you, O great mountain of human obstacles? Before
Zerubbabel, who with Joshua had led the return of the exiles from
Babylon and who was undertaking the rebuilding of the temple,
before him you shall become a plain, a mere mole hill! And he shall
bring forth the finishing gable stone of the new temple with loud
shoutings of the people, crying, Grace, grace to it! (Zech. 4:7)*

The temple will be rebuilt in Israel very shortly. Every
part for the new temple is stashed away somewhere in Israel.

According to a news item in the Sept/Oct 1974 issue of
Logos Journal,

> *Initial construction began this summer on the first large, central
> Jewish house of worship in the Holy City since the destruction of
> the Temple 1,904 years ago. Called the "Jerusalem Great
> Synagogue," the sanctuary will be a central, representative
> sanctuary to which Jewish pilgrims from all over the world may
> come to pray—just as they did to the Temple of old. . . . "No one is
> suggesting that this means the restoration of the Temple," [said]
> Rabbi Dr. Maurice A. Jaffee, "but there are parallels." Dr. Jaffee
> is president of the Union of Israel Synagogues which is sponsoring
> the project. Every Jew in the world is encouraged to contribute
> something to the expense of building the structure, just as were the
> Jews of old to contribute to building the original Temple.*
>
> *And there are other parallels. For instance, the "Great
> Synagogue" is being constructed of "radiant stone," as was that of*

the Temple of Bible times. It also is to be situated next to the head-quarters of Israel's rabbinical authority just as was the historic Temple. The building material is called "golden stone" and its color changes in the course of a day from gray to white to gold as the sun angles across the sky.

We know that this Temple must be built before Jesus' return, because this is where the anti-Christ will come in and say after three and a half years of Tribulation, "Worship me."

Moreover the word of the Lord came to me, saying, The hands of Zerubbabel have laid the foundations of this house; his hands shall also finish it. Then you shall know that the Lord of hosts has sent me, His messenger, to you. Who with reason despises the day of small things? For these seven shall rejoice when they see the plummet in the hand of Zerubbabel. These seven are the eyes of the Lord which run to and fro throughout the whole earth. (Zech. 4:8-10)

These seven eyes of the Lord are explained in the Book of Revelation:

And there between the throne and the four living creatures and among the elders of the heavenly, Sanhedrin, I saw a Lamb standing, as though it had been slain, with seven horns and with seven eyes, which are the seven Spirits of God, that is, the sevenfold Holy Spirit, Who have been sent into all the earth. (Rev. 5:6)

Jesus is the Lamb, the One with the seven manifold Spirit of God upon him, and the seven eyes of the Lord which run to and fro throughout all the earth, are the eyes of the Holy Spirit. The Holy Spirit is everywhere, He sees everything, He knows all things, If we step out of line, He convicts us, if we haven't rejected Him. He brings us back to the right path, again and again. We sometimes give up on Him, but He never gives up on us.

Then I said to him, What are these two olive trees on the right side of the lampstand and on the left side of it? And a second time I said

> *to him, What are these two olive branches which are beside the two golden tubes or spouts by which the golden oil is emptied out? And he answered me, Do you not know what these are? And I said, No, my lord. Then he said. These are the two sons of oil, Joshua the high priest and Zerubbabel the prince of Judah—the two anointed ones—who stand before the Lord of the whole earth as His anointed instruments. (Zech. 4:11-14)*

Zerubbabel was a living miracle, because when the people of Judah went into captivity, Nebuchadnezzar tried to stop the Messiah from coming into the world by killing the innocent babes. He knew there would be a Savior coming from the royal house of David, the royal house of Judah, so he killed all the princes and castrated the rest of the male children. But somehow, Nebuchadnezzar missed Zerubbabel. The Lord always has somebody tucked away into a little corner, a remnant hidden away. Zerubbabel was the one who would lead the captives back from Babylon into Jerusalem.

Now the Lord says that Joshua, the high priest, and Zerubbabel, the prince of Judah, would be pouring oil into the lamp. If the lamp was the light of the world, that means they would be filling the lamp with the Holy Spirit through the Word of God. They would be teaching the people. Joshua and Zerubbabel would feed the lamp, the lamp would glow all over the world, and the Word of God and the Holy Spirit would glorify Jesus Christ.

Then Zechariah had another vision:

> *Again I lifted up my eyes, and behold, I saw a scroll flying in the air. And the angel said to me, What do you see?*
> *And I answered, I see a flying scroll which is thirty feet long and fifteen feet wide.*
> *Then he said to me, This is the curse that goes out over the face of the whole land; for everyone who steals shall be cut off from henceforth according to it. I will bring the curse forth, says the Lord of hosts, and it shall enter the house of the thief, and into the house of him who swears falsely by My name; and it shall abide in*

the midst of his house and shall consume it, both its timber and its stones. (Zech. 5:1-4)

On this flying scroll were written curses against stealing, swearing, lying, cheating—anything that was unrighteous. And as the flying scroll went over all the land, it removed sin by destroying the sinner, consuming his house with fire.

That's a tough way to go, isn't it. The Lord says, "I hate the sin, but I love the sinner, but the sinner has failed to repent." The Lord has brought him under conviction many times, but he wants to stay in his sin. He enjoys staying in it, stealing, lying, cheating. And the Lord shows very clearly, in this vision to Zechariah, that in the end times He will remove the sin from among His unrepentant people by destroying the sinner. That's the only alternative left to Him. He's tried for years to bring them to the right path, but they have refused. The Body of believers, those who have repented and received Jesus, are already in heaven when this vision becomes reality.

> *Then the angel who talked with me came forward and said to me, Lift up now your eyes and see what this is that goes forth.*
> *And I said, What is it? What does it symbolize?*
> *And he said, This that goes forth is an ephah-like vessel for separate grains all collected together. This, he continued, is the symbol of the sinners mentioned above and is the resemblance of their iniquity throughout the whole land. (Zech. 5:5-6)*

Zechariah's sixth vision was of a flying ephah, a basket-like container which holds just a little over a bushel. The ephah was flying around, collecting grain, a symbol of the sinners who refused to repent.

> *Behold, a round, flat weight of lead was lifted, and there sat a woman in the midst of the ephah-like vessel. And he, the angel talking with me, said, This is lawlessness—wickedness! And he thrust*

> *her back into the ephah, and he cast the weight of lead upon the*
> *mouth of it! (Zech. 5:7)*

The woman represented sin and wickedness, because sin came into the world through a woman, when Eve paid more attention to the lies of a serpent than she paid to the truth of God. And the angel sealed the woman, wickedness, in the ephah with a weight of lead.

> *I lifted up my eyes, and looked, and behold, there were two women*
> *coming forward! The wind was in their wings, for they had wings*
> *like the wings of a stork, and they lifted up the ephah-like vessel*
> *between the earth and the heavens. Then said I to the angel who*
> *talked with me, Where are they taking the ephah, the bushel?*
> *And he said to me, To the land of Shinar, Babylonia, to build*
> *it a house, and when it is finished, to set up the ephah, the symbol*
> *of such sinners and their guilt, there upon its own base. (Zech.*
> *5:9-11)*

The spirit of Babylon, the spirit of sin, the spirit of Satan, is still with us. It will not be destroyed until the Second Coming. But just as sin and death came into the world through the instrument of a woman, so the only antidote to sin and death, Jesus, entered the world through the instrument of another woman.

> *And again I lifted up my eyes and saw, and behold, four chariots*
> *came out from between two mountains; and the mountains were*
> *mountains of firm, immovable bronze. The first chariot had red or*
> *bay horses, the second chariot had black horses, the third chariot*
> *had white horses, and the fourth chariot had dappled, active and*
> *strong horses. Then I said to the angel who talked with me, What*
> *are these, my lord?*
> *And the angel answered me, These are the four winds or*
> *spirits of the heavens, which go forth from presenting themselves*
> *before the Lord of all the earth. (Zech. 6:1-5)*

According to the Scripture, these four winds are angels:

*He will send out His angels with a loud trumpet call, and they will
gather His elect, His chosen ones, from the four winds, even from
one end of the universe to the other. (Matt. 24:31)*

In Psalm 104:4 we read that God makes winds His messengers, and flames of fire His ministers. The Lord used the
wind as His instrument, and the winds went forth from pre-
senting themselves before the Lord of all the earth to bring
judgment upon those who refused to come to the Lord. The
Lord brings hurricanes, typhoons—He uses the wind. God is
ruler over all the universe, nature is subject to Him. Nothing
happens by accident, only by His divine will and appointment.

*The chariot with the black horse is going forth into the north coun-
try. (Zech. 6:6a)*

The Lord will say to the north country, which is Russia, "I
have prepared a place for you in Zion. Move forward and go
into Zion. Nobody will be able to stop you." We're coming
very close to the time when the Lord will give that command.

*The white ones are going forth after them because there are two
northern powers to be overcome. (Zech. 6:6b)*

The other northern power to be overcome is China.

*And the dappled ones are going forth toward the south country.
And the chariot with the strong, red or bay horses went forth, and
they sought to go that they might patrol the earth. And the Lord
said to them, Go, walk to and fro through the earth and patrol it.
So they walked about through the earth, watching and protecting
it. (Zech. 6:6c-7)*

The red horses patrolling the earth symbolize the blood
of Jesus and His Holy Spirit bringing the sinners who would
repent home to the Lord Jesus Christ. At this point, those

who would not repent would be doomed. There would be no other time of salvation.

> *Then He summoned me and said, Behold, these that go toward the*
> *north country have quieted My Spirit of wrath, and they have*
> *caused it to rest in the north country. (Zech. 6:8)*

These that go toward the north country, Russia and China, have quieted His Spirit of wrath and judgment and caused it to rest in the north country because the people have submitted themselves to the will of the Lord. This tells us that even at the last moment, those who want to come to the Lord will be granted forgiveness. They will be granted a last-minute reprieve if they say, "Lord, forgive me of my sin. I repent, I accept You, Jesus, as my Savior."

> *And the word of the Lord came to me, saying, Accept donations*
> *and offerings from these as representatives of the exiles, from Hel-*
> *dai, from Tobijah, from Jedaiah; and you come the same day and*
> *go to the house of Josiah the son of Zephaniah, where they have*
> *come from Babylon. Yes, take from them silver and gold, and make*
> *crowns and set one upon the head of Joshua the son of Jehozadak,*
> *the high priest. And say to him, Thus says the Lord of hosts: You,*
> *Joshua behold, look at, keep in sight, watch the Man, the Messiah,*
> *whose name is the Branch; for He shall grow up in His place, He*
> *shall build the true temple of the Lord. (Zech. 6:9-12)*

The message to all of Israel, to all of the world through Joshua, the high priest, was to watch and wait and look for the Branch, the Messiah who is coming, for He shall build a true temple of the Lord.

> *Yes, you are building a temple of the Lord, but it is He Who shall*
> *build the true temple of the Lord, and He shall bear the honor and*
> *glory as of the only begotten of the Father, and He shall sit and*
> *rule upon His throne. And He shall be a priest upon His throne,*
> *and the counsel of peace shall be between the two offices, Priest and*
> *King. (Zech. 6:13)*

Jesus fulfills this prophecy saying He would be Priest and King:

> *And the Word, Christ, became flesh, human, incarnate, and tabernacled. He fixed His tent of flesh, lived awhile among us, and we actually saw His glory, His honor, His majesty; such glory as an only begotten son receives from his father, full of grace, favor, loving kindness, and truth. (John 1:14)*

In John we read the prayer of Jesus:

> *And now, Father, glorify Me along with Yourself and restore Me to such majesty and honor in Your presence as I had with You before the world existed. (John 17:5)*

Further, in Paul's writing to the Hebrews, we read:

> *But we are able to see Jesus, Who was ranked lower than the angels for a little while, crowned with glory and honor because of His having suffered death, in order that by the grace–unmerited favor–of God to us sinners, He might experience death for every individual person. (Heb. 2:9)*

We don't have to experience death, because Jesus has already done it for us. We may go through the door of death, but death has lost its sting. We have nothing to fear, because Christ Jesus is waiting on the other side of that door. And He'll take us to God the Father and say, "This is one of Mine. I want to present him to You. He's an heir with Me in Your kingdom. I have already prepared a place for him."

> *The other crown shall be credited to Helem (Heldai), and to Tobijah, and to Jedaiah, and to the kindness and favor of Josiah the son of Zephaniah, and shall be in the temple of the Lord for a reminder and memorial. (Zech. 6:14)*

The earthly crown will be worn by the earthly king, but the heavenly crown will be worn by Jesus Christ, the spiritual

King. And at His Second Coming, the earthly and the
spiritual will be united together, and there will be only one
crown remaining.

> *And those who are far off shall come and help build the temple of*
> *the Lord, and you shall know that the Lord has sent me, Zechariah,*
> *to you. And your part in this shall come to pass, if you will dili-*
> *gently obey the voice of the Lord your God. (Zech. 6:15)*

There's that big *if* covenant again. You shall take part in
this that shall come to pass *if* you will diligently obey God. A
Christian has to lead a consistent life. He's got to stop being
like a Yo-Yo. A consistent life in Christ Jesus is a balanced life
in Him, going from one degree of glory to another and not
backsliding.

Chapter 4

Zechariah 7-10

In the fourth year of the reign of King Darius, the word of the Lord came to Zechariah on the fourth day of the ninth month, Chislev. Now the people of Bethel had sent Sharezer and Regemmelech and their men, to pray and entreat the favor of the Lord, and to speak to the priests of the house of the Lord of hosts, and to the prophets, saying, Now that I have returned from exile, should I weep in the fifth month, separating myself, as I have done these so many years in Babylonia? (Zech. 7:1-3)

On a recent tour in Israel, we had to change our itinerary one day because it was the time of weeping for the destruction of the temple. We went to Hebron instead of to Jerusalem that day because in Jerusalem, everybody was sitting on the floor weeping. Even in Hebron, people were sitting on the floor in sackcloth and ashes, mourning at the tomb of Jacob over the destruction of the temple. Although they were returned from exile, they were still weeping.

Then came the word of the Lord of hosts to me, Zechariah, saying, Speak to all the people of the land and to the priests, saying, When you fasted and mourned in the fifth and in the seventh months,

51

> *even those seventy years you were in exile, was it for Me that you*
> *fasted, for Me? (Zech. 7:4-5)*

That is a very good question, "Did you fast for Me?" And
the answer is, "No, Lord. We didn't fast for you. We fasted
because we felt sorry for ourselves, that we lost our grand and
glorious temple." Today, the Lord still asks, "Do you fast out
of love for Me? Or are you a bunch of hypocrites, weeping
and praying all over the place just so your fellowman can see
you?"

Next, the Lord had more questions to ask:

> *And when you eat and when you drink, do you not eat for your-*
> *selves and drink for yourselves? Should you not hear the words*
> *which the Lord cried by the former prophets, when Jerusalem was*
> *inhabited and in prosperity, with her cities round about her, and*
> *the South and the lowlands were inhabited? And the word of the*
> *Lord came to Zechariah, saying, Thus has the Lord of hosts spo-*
> *ken: Execute true judgment, and show mercy and kindness and*
> *tender compassion every man to his brother; And oppress not the*
> *widow, or the fatherless, the temporary resident, or the poor, And*
> *let none of you devise or imagine or think evil against his brother*
> *in your heart. (Zech. 7:6-10)*

The Lord of hosts has spoken; He says there's something
better than fasting, that true judgment involves showing
compassion. The Lord had told them what to do,

> *But they refused to listen, and turned a rebellious and stubborn*
> *shoulder, and made heavy and dull their ears, that they might not*
> *hear. Yes, they made their heart as an adamant stone or a diamond*
> *point. (Zech. 7:11-12a)*

A diamond point cuts everything else, but it can't be cut
itself except with special tools. When the Israelites made their
hearts as a diamond point, nobody could reach them. They
had hardened their hearts. And as the love, and grace, and
mercy of God was showered upon them, they became harder

and harder, refusing the message that God was bringing them. They had done this, God said,

> *lest they should hear the law and the words which the Lord of hosts had sent by His Spirit through the former prophets. Therefore there came great wrath from the Lord of hosts. So it came to pass that as He cried, and they would not hear, He said, So they shall cry, and I will not answer, says the Lord of hosts. (Zech. 7:12b-13)*

This is a vital lesson for all Christians, not just for the people of Israel. The Lord says, in effect, "If I cannot remove the sin through your repentance, then I'll remove the sin by removing you. If you continue to ignore Me, I'll ignore you." In the New Testament, we find the same kind of warning repeated:

> *It is impossible to restore and bring again to repentance those who have been once for all enlightened, who have consciously tasted the heavenly gift, and have become sharers of the Holy Spirit, and have felt how good the Word of God is and the mighty powers of the age and the world to come, if they then deviate from the faith and turn away from their allegiance; it is impossible to bring them back to repentance, for . . . they nail upon the cross the Son of God afresh, as far as they are concerned, and are holding Him up to contempt and shame and public disgrace. For the soil which has drunk the rain that repeatedly falls upon it, and produces vegetation useful for those for whose benefit it is cultivated, partakes of a blessing from God. But if that same soil persistently bears thorns and thistles, it is considered worthless and near to being cursed, whose end is to be burned. (Heb. 6:4-8)*

> *If we go on deliberately and willingly sinning after once acquiring the knowledge of the Truth, there is no longer any sacrifice left to to atone for our sins—no further offering to which to look forward. There is nothing left for us then but a kind of awful and fearful prospect and expectation of divine judgment and the fury of burning wrath and indignation which will consume those who put themselves in opposition to God. (Heb. 10:26-31)*

God says if we constantly and deliberately keep on sinning against Him, there's no longer any sacrifice left. He said to the Israelites, "Because you Israelites have refused My love and My grace and mercy, here's what I will do:

> *I will scatter them with a whirlwind among all the nations whom they know not and who know not them. Thus the land was desolate after they had gone, so that no man passed through or returned; for they, the Jews by their sins, had caused to be laid waste and forsaken the pleasant land, the land of desire.*
>
> *And the word of the Lord of hosts came to me, Zechariah, saying, Thus says the Lord of hosts: I am jealous, I am righteously indignant, for Zion with great jealousy, and I am righteously indignant for her with great wrath against her enemies. Thus says the Lord: I shall return to Zion, and will dwell in the midst of Jerusalem; and Jerusalem shall be called the faithful city of truth, and the mountain of the Lord of hosts, the holy mountain. (Zech. 7:14-8:3)*

Jerusalem will finally be called the city of truth because Jesus will come and dwell there. He will return back to the very same mount that He ascended from, the Mount of Olives.

> *Thus says the Lord of hosts: Old men and old women shall again dwell in Jerusalem and sit out in the streets, every man with his staff in his hand for very advanced age. And the streets of the city shall be full of boys and girls playing in its streets. (Zech. 8:4-5)*

The Lord says the city of Jerusalem would be full of not just kids but old people in advanced age, every man with his staff in his hand, ready to move at a moment's notice.

> *Thus says the Lord of hosts: Because it will be marvelous in the eyes of the remnant of this people in those days in which it comes to pass, should it also be marvelous in My eyes? says the Lord of hosts. (Zech 8:6)*

The Lord is speaking about the Second Coming of Jesus.

It will be marvelous in everybody's eyes. Today, men would say that it would be impossible for boys and girls to play in the streets of Jerusalem in safety and for old men and old women to sit out in the streets in advanced old age without harm. But what is impossible with men is possible with God.

> *Thus says the Lord of hosts: Behold, I will save My people from the east country, from the west, the country of the going down of the sun. And I will bring them home, and they shall dwell in the midst of Jerusalem. They shall be My people, and I will be their God, in truth and faithfulness and in righteousness. (Zech. 8:7-8)*

This is the Gospel of the Old Testament that the people of Israel were to go out and preach to all nations: "I will be your God and you shall be My people." But they failed to do it.

He said, "Don't be afraid to go in. I'll give you power from on high. You'll move by My Spirit. I'll give you the right words at the right time and the right place to bring what is necessary, to plant a seed on fertile ground—in a heart I have prepared."

The Lord says, "I will be their God in truth, in faithfulness, and in righteousness" Jesus said, "I am the Way, I am the Truth, and I am the Life." If He is the way, we know how to go in the right way—by following Him. And if He is the truth, His truth sets us free from all our hangups. And we remain free in Him if we stay in a state of repentance, in a state of walking with the Lord in His truth and in His righteousness.

> *Thus says the Lord of hosts: Let your hands be strong and hardened, you who in these days hear these words from the mouth of the prophets, who on the day that the foundation of the house of the Lord of hosts was laid, foretold that the temple should be rebuilt. (Zech. 8:9)*

The temple was rebuilt once, but, as I mentioned earlier,

there's another temple about to be rebuilt, right now.

> *For before those days, there was no hire for man, nor any hire for beast, neither was there any peace of success to him who went out or came in, because of the adversary and the oppressor; for I set—let loose—all men, every one against his neighbor. (Zech. 8:10)*

In the last days, men and horses will be out of work. Early in the twentieth century, horses became unemployed, and today, the other part of this prophecy is taking place. Men are losing their jobs. We have the largest amount of unemployment among men in our history. Women can get jobs because they will work for half the pay men require. But men are out of work.

The Lord says that He Himself set men against each other, letting the adversary loose, to attack His people. Why would Satan be allowed to attack us? To draw us back to God. To let the Lord establish Himself in men. To let men be established in the Lord. We have all been given a measure of faith, and by causing an attack to come upon us, the Lord builds up our faith. He'll lead us from faith to faith until we reach that point of perfection He designed for us—and designed us for—to be just like Jesus Christ, who enables us to withstand big temptation when it comes along, to meet the big test.

God is still sovereign. Satan himself can move only by the will of God who will allow him to move only so far.

Look at Job. Satan came before God and said, "Big deal. Your man Job—sure he's faithful, sure he's loyal. You give him wealth, and flocks, and a wife, and kids, and cars, and swimming pools— Naturally, he'll worship, praise, and thank You all day long. But let me have a little nip at him and see what happens."

The Lord said, "I know Job. He'll still praise Me in spite of everything." And then He told Satan he could do anything he wanted to do to Job, but not to touch his life. It was like they had a little bet on, to see how Job would react.

Satan was not able to break Job's spirit, because Job was moving in the Spirit of the Lord. Job's friends came upon the scene and told him to give up, to take the easy way out. They asked him why he was fighting this thing out. It'd be easier to die and give up.

"You know you're going to be with the Lord, Job. Why are you still struggling?" No matter how they urged him, Job said, "I will still praise and thank God." And he did. As a result, Job's ending was greater than his beginning.

Know for a certainty that your ending and my ending is going to be greater than our beginning, too—because Jesus died for us. He went to the cross for us, and made us heirs with Him of the promise of eternal life.

Again we see the Lord speaking to the people of Israel through the prophet Zechariah:

> *But now in this period, since you began to build, I am not to the remnant of this people as in the former days, says the Lord of hosts. For there shall be the seed sowing of peace and prosperity; the vine shall yield her fruit, and the ground shall give its increase, and the heavens shall give their dew; and I will cause the remnant of this people to inherit and possess all these things. (Zech. 8:11-12)*

God says that only a remnant of His people Israel will be saved.

Is there a conflict between what the Holy Spirit says here through Zechariah and what the Holy Spirit says through Paul in Romans 11:26: "And so all Israel will be saved?" No, there's no conflict: During this time of the outpouring of the Holy Spirit, God will move by His Spirit, and those who come to the Lord Jesus Christ, as they are doing by the thousands in Israel, will go up in the Rapture as you and I will. They'll know the Lord Jesus Christ, and they'll be taken up for the marriage supper of the Lamb. But the ones who have hardened their hearts will remain, and we see that even out of that group God still has a remnant. One-third of them will accept the Lord Jesus Christ (Zech. 13:9); two-thirds will reject Him even as He stands in glory on the Mount of Olives.

> *And as you have been a curse and a byword among the nations, O house of Judah and house of Israel, so will I save you, and you shall be a blessing. Fear not, but let your hands be strong and hardened. (Zech. 8:13)*

This is the same message that God gave to Joshua and to the people of Israel in the days of Joshua. "Be strong and of good courage. Have the courage and the strength to believe Me for My word." When He says, "Fear not, I am with you; I'll never leave you nor forsake you," have the courage and the tenacity to hang on.

We're attached to Him. He may dangle us over a cliff for a while, but we're tied to Him. We can't fall; He's not going to drop us.

Can we thank Him while we're hanging over that cliff? The dangling is supposed to teach us how far we can trust Him. And we learn that our Daddy is absolutely trustworthy. It's as simple as that.

> *For thus says the Lord of hosts: As I thought to bring calamity upon you, when your fathers provoked Me to wrath, says the Lord of hosts, and I did not relent or revoke your sentence, So again have I purposed in these last days to do good to Jerusalem and to the house of Judah. Fear not! (Zech. 8:14-15)*

The Lord has purposed to do good to us in these end times, by His own grace, and His mercy. There's no reason for us to be afraid.

> *These are the things that you shall do: speak every man the truth with his neighbor; to render the truth, and pronounce the judgment or verdict that makes for peace in the courts at your gates. And let none of you think or imagine or devise evil or injury in*

your hearts against his neighbor, and love no false oath, for all
these things I hate, says the Lord. (Zech. 8:16-17)

If you think evil against your neighbor in your heart, you
have actually committed that evil against him. You don't have
to carry it out. You thought it. You felt it, and that makes you
as guilty as if you'd done the deed itself.

And the word of the Lord of hosts came to me, Zechariah, saying,
Thus says the Lord of hosts: The fast of the fourth month, and the
fast of the fifth month, and the fast of the seventh month, and the
fast of the tenth, shall be to the house of Judah times of joy and
gladness, and cheerful appointed seasons; therefore, in order that
this may happen to you, as the condition of fulfilling the promise,
love truth and peace. (Zech. 8:18-19)

The Lord says, "You have been fasting for yourself in sitting on the floor and mourning for the temple which was destroyed, but the day is coming when you will fast for the Lord,
and it will be a fast of joy."

Do Christians know how to fast rightfully? Yes, because
when the Lord lays it upon our hearts to fast for Him, we do it
joyfully. During the years I was a Jewish rabbi and before I
recognized that Jesus was the Messiah, I fasted one day out of
the year, on the Day of Atonement, but not without walking
around so mournfully that everybody knew that I was fasting.
Jesus said, "You're doing it for yourself. You're doing it so
your fellowman knows you're fasting, but you aren't even receiving the glory. Your fellowman could care less what kind of
a kook you are. Wait to receive praise and honor from Me. I'll
give it to you."

Before I was ordained as a Christian minister at Melodyland Christian Center, the Lord led me to fast for three days
and nights. It wasn't a long time, but I enjoyed it. It was in
peace, love, and joy. The time flew by, and I didn't mind at all.
But as a rabbi, I was never once able to fast from sundown to

sundown. I would sneak out during the service and get a hotdog—while the cantor was chanting the song. I couldn't even fast with mourning, let alone with joy.

> *Thus says the Lord of hosts: It shall yet come to pass, that there shall come to Jerusalem peoples and the inhabitants of many and great cities. And the inhabitants of one city shall go to them of another, saying, Let us go speedily to pray and entreat the favor of the Lord, and to seek, inquire of and require, to meet our own most essential need, the Lord of hosts. I will go also. (Zech. 8:20-21)*

When the Lord was here the first time, needy people came to Him and He always met their needs. Today, we are still a needy people (if we are honest), and He still meets every need. And so it will be in the end times, at His Second Coming. Many people of all nations will go up to Jerusalem to entreat the favor of the Lord, to ask something from Him:

> *Yes, many people and strong nations shall come to Jerusalem to seek, to inquire of and require, to fill their own urgent need, the Lord of hosts, and to pray to the Lord for His favor. Thus says the Lord of hosts: In those days, ten men, out of all languages of the nations, shall take hold of the robe of him who is a Jew, saying, Let us go with you, for we have heard that God is with you. (Zech. 8:22-23)*

The Jew here is one who is part of that remnant that knows the Lord, a completed Jew. Ten heathens who do not know Jesus Christ will grab hold of the Jew's robe and say, "Come, let us go with you, because you know the Lord."

In chapter 9, a burden is given to Zechariah:

> *The burden or oracle, the thing to be lifted up, of the word of the Lord is against the land of Hadrach in Syria, and Damascus shall be its resting place, for the Lord has an eye upon mankind as upon all the tribes of Israel; and Hamath also which borders on Damascus, Tyre with Sidon, though they are very wise. And Tyre has built herself a stronghold on an island, a half mile from the shore, which seems impregnable, and heaped up silver like dust, and fine*

> *gold like the mire of the streets. Behold, the Lord will cast her out and dispossess her; He will smite her power in the sea and into it, and Tyre shall be devoured by fire.*
>
> *The strong cities of Philistia shall see it, and fear; Ashkelon, Gaza also, and be sorely pained; Ekron, for her confidence and expectation shall be put to shame; and a king, a monarchial government, shall perish from Gaza, and Ashkelon shall not be inhabited. And a mongrel people shall dwell in Ashod, and I will put an end to the pride of the Philistines. I will take out of the Philistine's mouth and from between his teeth the abominable idolatrous sacrifices eaten with the blood. And he, too, shall remain and be a remnant for our God, and he shall be as a chieftain, the head over a thousand, in Judah, and Ekron shall be like one of the Jebusites who at last were merged and had lost their identity in Israel. (Zech. 9:1-7)*

The Lord says that even from the Philistines there will be a remnant who will come to know the Lord Jesus Christ. The Philistines are a mixture of the original people of Canaan, the Amorites, the Hittites, with the Arabs, the Moabites, and Ammonites. And today, it's much easier to preach the Gospel to them than to anybody else. Their hearts have been prepared.

> *Then I will encamp about My house as a guard or a garrison, so that none shall march back and forth; and no oppressor or demanding collector shall again over-run them, for now My eyes are upon them. Rejoice greatly, O daughter of Zion! Shout aloud, O daughter of Jerusalem! Lo, your King comes to you; He is uncompromisingly just, and having salvation—triumphant and victorious; patient, meek, lowly and riding on a donkey, upon a colt, the foal of a donkey. (Zech. 9:8-9)*

This prophecy was fulfilled in John 12:14-15 at the first coming of Jesus Christ. No ordinary man could ride upon a colt, the foal of a donkey that had never been ridden before. He would be like a bucking bronco. In half a second, we'd be thrown off. But Jesus rode upon a colt with no trouble. And this King of kings, this Lord of lords, had salvation in His hands.

> *And I will cut off and exterminate the war chariot from Ephraim,*
> *and the war horse from Jerusalem, and the battle-bow shall be cut*
> *off; and He, the Lord, shall speak the word, and peace shall come*
> *to the nations. His dominion shall be from the Mediterranean Sea*
> *to any other sea, and from the River Euphrates to the ends of the*
> *earth! As for you also, because of and for the sake of the covenant*
> *of the Lord with His people which was sealed with sprinkled cov-*
> *enant blood, I have released and sent forth your imprisoned people*
> *out of the waterless pit. (Zech. 9:10-11)*

This promise of the release of prisoners from the water-less pit—from hell—was fulfilled by Jesus Christ.

In Luke 4:16-19 we read that Jesus went to the synagogue in Nazareth as was His custom on every Sabbath morning, and He was handed the scrolls of Isaiah. He un-rolled the scroll to the sixty-first chapter and read,

> *The Spirit of the Lord is upon me, because He has anointed me to*
> *preach the good news. He has sent Me to set the captives free. (Isa.*
> *61:1)*

Jesus did set the captives free, just as Zechariah had prophesied, for the sake of the covenant which was sealed with sprinkled covenant blood. This covenant was given to the Israelites as they stood before Mount Sinai and the Lord spoke the ten commandments to the people. Then the Lord told Moses to seal the covenant by taking the blood of a lamb and sprinkling it upon the people of Israel. This sprinkled covenant blood was a symbol of the blood of Jesus Christ. And Jesus not only released us, but He went down into hell—the waterless pit—and preached the Gospel and set the captives free from that place (I Pet. 3:18-20).

> *Turn you to the stronghold of security and prosperity, you prison-*

*ers of hope; even today do I declare that I will restore double your
former prosperity to you. (Zech. 9:12)*

We are to turn our eyes upon Him who is our stronghold
of security and *prosperity*. He did not say, "I have come into
the world to give you a life of poverty." He said, "I have come
into the world to give you life, and to give it to you more
abundantly than you've ever had it before."

Jesus wants us to have a good life. What better witness for
Him than to possess abundant life and not let that abundance
take hold of us. Sin lies not in wealth but in our grasping for it
so that it becomes our love instead of Jesus. The blessing that
God gave to the people of Israel through the high priest,
"May the Lord bless you and keep you," implies, "May He
bless you in all material possessions, and may He keep you
from being possessed by the blessing that He gives you." We
are not to be possessed by God's blessing, but to possess it and
use it for His praise, honor, and glory.

> *For I have bent Judah for me as My bow, filled the bow with E-
> phraim as My arrow, and will stir up your sons, O Zion, against
> your sons, O Greece, and will make you, Israel, as the sword of a
> mighty man. (Zech. 9:13)*

This prophecy was fulfilled a long time ago in history
when Alexander the Great invaded and subdued Israel.

> *And the Lord shall be seen over them, and His arrow shall go forth
> as the lightning. And the Lord God will blow the trumpet, and will
> go forth in the windstorms of the south. The Lord of hosts shall
> defend and protect them. (Zech. 9:14-15a)*

The battle is the Lord's; it always is. If you or I have a
problem, it belongs to God.

Many of us like to play the part of Jesus. I used to think I
was cast for His role; I carried everybody else's problems, as
well as my own, until Jesus showed me what a usurper I was.

"Why do you try to do it, when I'm standing here?"

Many of us come forward in response to an altar call and say, "Jesus, I'm giving You all my problems, burdens, and needs," but then we retrieve them and walk out as burdened as ever. We feel naked without them. But let the Lord do it. If He does it, you know it's going to be done right.

> *They shall devour and they shall tread on their fallen enemies as on sling stones that have missed their aim. They shall drink of victory and be noisy and turbulent as if they were drunk from wine, and become full like bowls used to catch the sacrificial blood, like the corners of the sacrificial altar. And the Lord their God will save them on that day as the flock of His people, for they shall be as the precious jewels of a crown, lifted high over and shining glitteringly upon His land. For how great is God's goodness, and how great is His beauty! And how great He will make Israel's goodliness and Israel's beauty! Grain shall make the young men thrive, and fresh wine the maidens. (Zech. 9:15b-17)*

This is a picture of the Second Coming of Christ, the victorious, beautiful, abundant life. How great is the Lord, how good He is, how faithful He is in keeping His everlasting promise!

There is a further picture of the beauty of Israel in the writing of the prophet Isaiah:

> *The wilderness and the dry land shall be glad, the desert shall rejoice and blossom as the rose and the autumn crocus. (Isa. 35:1)*

Where will the water come from to make the desert blossom like a rose? The Orthodox rabbis believe that beneath Israel is an underground river. You can tap into it by following the directions in the Bible, and the land will flourish like a rose.

Even unbelievers take the Word of God literally in some areas. But where it talks about a coming Messiah or the Second Coming of Christ, where God says literally that they will look upon Him whom they have pierced, unbelievers don't accept it. "God is speaking in allegory," they say.

I remember Louis Evans, Sr., standing up to preach at the Hollywood Presbyterian Church. He started with Genesis, with the Garden of Eden.

"We really don't believe that story, do we?" he said. So he tore the story of Adam and Eve out of the Bible. He continued going clear through the whole Bible that way until the only thing left in his Bible was the begats. And then he turned to the people and said, "In the name of the Lord Jesus Christ, I want to see how far you can get with the begats. We just tore out all the promises of God in His Word, just as modern liberal Christianity has done. They have reduced the Bible to the begats." Pastor Evans demonstrated that day very clearly that you can't tear one page out of the Word of God without tearing out the whole thing. But there are seventy-seven hundred promises in this book that belong to you and me. And no man can take them away from us. Praise God.

> *Ask of the Lord rain in the time of the latter or spring rain. It is the Lord Who makes lightnings, which usher in the rain and give men showers of it, to every one grass in the field. (Zech. 10:11)*

This latter rain for which we are to ask the Lord is the outpouring of the Holy Spirit. And He promises that just as an earthly father doesn't give his child a stone when he asks for bread, so He will give us the Holy Spirit when we ask for it. And with the Holy Spirit, He gives us a special dividend, a very special language to use when we talk to Him, when we pray to Him, when we worship Him. It's very mysterious— and marvelous in our eyes.

> *For the idols have spoken vanity, emptiness, falsity, and futility, and the diviners have seen a lie, and the dreamers have told false dreams; they comfort in vain. (Zech. 10:2a)*

Recently I was thrilled to see a signboard in front of a church which said, very boldly, "Satan does not care who or what you worship as long as it's not God." Anything that comes between you and the Lord is an idol. And idolatry is empty, a dream, vanity. The Living God is real.

> *The people go their way like sheep, they are afflicted and hurt because there is no shepherd. (Zech. 10:2b)*

A shepherd never drives his sheep, he leads them. He moves, and the sheep follow him. If Christians have no shepherd, they go astray. They turn to their own way. But Jesus is the Good Shepherd, who laid down His life for His sheep. We know His voice and we follow Him. Everything else is vanity. Everything else is false.

Where there's no shepherd to show them the way, the truth, and the life, the sheep are afflicted and hurt.

> *Now, the Lord said, My anger is kindled against the shepherds who are not true shepherds, and I will punish the goat-leaders; for the Lord of hosts has visited His flock, the house of Judah, and will make them as His beautiful and majestic horse in the day of battle. (Zech. 10:3)*

God will punish those who teach what is not in the Word of God. Any shepherd, pastor, or teacher has to be careful that he doesn't manipulate the Word of God. In II Timothy 3 we are warned that in the end times there will be false teachers arriving upon the scene to lead the people astray. But the Lord has given us a standard to judge by. If a teaching does not conform to the Scripture, our suspicions ought to be alerted. Further, learn to listen for the response of the Holy Spirit within when you are listening to a teacher or preacher.

> *Out of him, out of the tribe of Judah, shall come the cornerstone,*

*out of him the tent peg, out of him the battle bow; every ruler shall
proceed from him. (Zech. 10:4)*

The building is laid upon a cornerstone. A peg holds up
the tent. Jesus is the cornerstone, the tent peg. This is a
prophecy about the first coming of Jesus. And if every ruler
proceeds from Jesus Christ, we cannot go against any authority, because it is of God.

> *They shall be as mighty men, treading down their enemies in the
> mire of the streets in the battle; and they shall fight, because the
> Lord is with them, and the oppressor's riders on horses shall be con-
> founded and put to shame. (Zech. 10:5)*

This is a picture of the last battle, the battle of Armageddon. The valley of Armageddon is thirty-five miles wide and a
hundred miles long. Every general who has looked at it has
agreed that it is an ideal place to have a battle. Russia has prepared the largest horse army in the world, ready to move at a
moment's notice to go into this valley and fight the final battle.

The vultures are already circling in the Valley of the Armageddon. God's preparing a feast for seven months for
these vultures to feed upon. And a new breed of vulture has
appeared in Israel, a breed never seen before. These vultures
are multiplying at three times the normal rate in Israel. This
is a sign of the end times.

And the Lord says,

> *I will strengthen the house of Judah, and I will save the house of
> Joseph (Ephraim). I will bring them back and cause them to dwell
> securely; for I have mercy, loving-kindness, and compassion.
>   They shall be as though I had not cast them off, for I am the
> Lord their God, and I will hear them. (Zech. 10:6)*

Many of us seem to think that Israel has been cut off. But
the Lord has never canceled His covenant. His covenant

promises are irrevocable, just as His gifts are irrevocable. He is going to hear Israel once again.

For a short while, God would not hear them, but now He is listening again. The age of the Gentiles is about to close, the age of the Jews is about to open. The acceptable time of the Lord is now. The Lord is about to move by His Spirit among the people of Israel, to save them. They will have an opportunity to know the Lord Jesus Christ as their Savior. If they turn to Him in repentance, He will forgive. It will be just as if He had never cast them off.

> *Then Ephraim, the ten tribes, shall become like a mighty warrior, and their hearts shall rejoice as through wine. Yes, their children shall see it and rejoice. Their hearts shall feel great delight and glory triumphantly in the Lord! I will hiss for them as the keeper does for his bees and gather them in, for I have redeemed them—I have purchased them with my body and blood—and they shall increase again as they have increased in Egypt. (Zech 10:7-8)*

Ephraim will rejoice, not from wine, but from the new Spirit within them, God's Holy Spirit.

> *And though I sow them among the nations, yet they shall earnestly remember Me in far countries, and with their children they shall live and shall return to God and the land He gave them. I will bring them, all Israel, home again from the land of Egypt, and gather them out of Assyria; and I will bring them into the land on the east and on the west of Jordan, into Gilead and Lebanon; and room enough shall not be found for them. And the Lord will pass through the sea of distress and affliction at the head of His people, as He did at the Red Sea. (Zech. 10:9-11a)*

It was Christ Jesus Himself who went before the people of Israel when they were going through the Red Sea. The pillar of cloud in front of them, the pillar of fire behind them. The Holy Spirit behind them and Jesus in front of them.

> *He will smite down the waves of the sea, and all the depths of the*

river Nile shall be dried up and put to shame; and the arrogance of Assyria shall be brought down, and the scepter or rod of the taskmasters of Egypt shall pass away. And I will strengthen Israel in the Lord, and they shall walk up and down and glory in His name, says the Lord. (Zech. 10:11b-12)

Israel will glory in the name of Jesus. They will say, "Jesus, thank You for going through this sea of affliction with us. Thank You that You've been with us all along. You have never forsaken us nor deserted us. But You've put us in a school to teach us that there's only one way we can stand and that is in You. By ourselves, we would always revert to the dust from which we came. Thank You, Lord Jesus Christ, that You died for us. We will praise You from this day forth."

Chapter 5

Zechariah 11-14

Open your doors, O Lebanon, that the fire may devour your cedars! Wail, O fir tree and cypress, for the cedar has fallen; because the glorious and lofty trees are laid waste! Wail, O you oaks of Bashan, for the thick and inaccessible forest on the steep mountain side has in flames been felled. A voice of the wailing of the shepherds! For their glory, the broad pasturage, is laid waste! A voice of the roaring of young lions. For the pride of the Jordan, the jungle, or thickets, is ruined! Thus says the Lord my God: Shepherd the flock destined for slaughter. Whose buyers or possessors slay them and hold themselves not guilty; and they who sell them say, Blessed be the Lord, for I have become rich! (Zech. 11:1-5a)

In Israel, there will be shepherds leading the flock destined for slaughter. God knows that two-thirds of Israel will reject Jesus as their Messiah. They are destined for slaughter. Their shepherds will say, "I have become rich because I have led them to their final destination."

And their own shepherds neither pity nor spare them from the wolves. (Zech. 11:5b)

The rest of the shepherds, who are supposed to be re-

71

sponsible for the flock of Israel, will stand by and say, "I will have nothing to do with them, because I don't want to get involved. I'll just stand by and see what happens." This has been the story of Israel all along. Nobody wants to get involved. Now the Lord says,

> *For I will no more pity or spare the inhabitants of the land, says the Lord; but lo, I will deliver every man into his neighbor's hand, into the hand of his foreign king. The enemy shall lay waste the land, and I will not deliver the people out of the hand of the foreign oppressor.*
>
> *So I, Zechariah, shepherded the flock of slaughter, truly the most miserable of the sheep. I took two shepherd's staffs, the one called Beauty or Grace, and the other I called Bands or Union; and I fed and shepherded the flock. I cut off the three shepherds— the civil authorities, the priests, and the prophets—in one month, for I was weary and impatient with them, and they also loathed me.*
>
> *So I, Zechariah, said, I will not be your shepherd. What is to die, let it die, and what is to be destroyed, let it be destroyed; and let the survivors devour one another's flesh. And I took my staff, Beauty or Grace, and broke it in pieces, to show that I was annulling the covenant or agreement which I had made with all the peoples not to molest them. So the covenant was annulled on that day, and thus the most wretched of the flock and the traffickers in the sheep, who were watching me, knew—recognized and understood—that it was truly the word of the Lord. (Zech. 11:6-11)*

Here was the covenant broken.

> *And I said to them, If it seems just and right to you, give me my wages; but if not, withhold them. So they weighed out for my price thirty pieces of silver. And the Lord said to me, Cast it to the potter! as if He said, To the dogs! the munificently miserable sum at which I and My shepherd am priced by them! And I, Zechariah, took the thirty pieces of silver, and I cast them to the potter in the house of the Lord. (Zech. 11:12-13)*

This is a foreshadowing of the one coming from the tribe of Dan who would be the betrayer of Christ for thirty pieces of silver.

We find the parallel in Matthew:

> *Then one of the twelve apostles, who was called Judas Iscariot, went to the chief of priests and said, What are you willing to give me if I hand Him over to you? And they weighed out and paid him thirty pieces of silver, about twenty-one dollars and sixty cents. (Matt. 26:14-15)*

That's all our Lord was worth, twenty-one dollars and sixty cents.

You know the rest of the story, but what would have happened to Judas if he had gone back to Jesus after the betrayal and said, "Lord, forgive me." Would there have been forgiveness?

Yes, praise God, there would have been forgiveness. But Judas made the mistake of going back to the law, to the priests, to the scribes, and he asked them to take the money back. But it was too late. He went to the wrong people.

> *Then I broke into pieces my other staff, Bands or Union, indicating that I was annulling the brotherhood between Judah and Israel. (Zech. 11:14)*

The old covenant which bound Judah and Israel to the Lord was annulled, making way for the new covenant to come into being.

> *And the Lord said to me, Take up once more the implements—the staff and rod of a shepherd—but this time of a worthless and wicked shepherd. For lo, I will raise up a false shepherd in the land. The lost and the perishing he will not miss or visit, the young and scattered he will not go to seek, the wounded and broken he will not heal, nor will he feed those that are sound and strong; but he will eat the flesh of the fat ones and he will break off their hoofs to consume all the flesh. Woe to the worthless and foolish shepherd who deserts the flock! The sword shall smite his arm and his right eye; his arm shall be utterly withered and his right eye utterly blinded. (Zech. 11:15-17)*

The Lord will raise up a false shepherd. In the New Testament, the false shepherd is a hireling, the anti-Christ. He will not feed those who are hungry. He will not heal those who are sick. He will not take care of anything. Instead, he will come riding in on the god of money that people have a tendency to worship. And when the ravening wolf comes, he will not lay down his life for the sheep, but he will desert the flock.

Why will the Lord permit such a thing to happen? Because the spirit of Babylon will have to be dealt with. We have to repent, to change our ways. We have to ask His forgiveness.

After these things, Zechariah received another burden of the Lord:

> *The burden or oracle–the thing to be lifted up–of the word of the Lord concerning Israel. Thus says the Lord, Who stretches out the heavens and lays the foundation of the earth and forms the spirit of man within him. (Zech. 12:1)*

God forms the spirit of man within every man. The heathen, every creature on the face of the earth, know that God is God. God took a piece of dust and clay, and man became a living soul by the breath of God. Every creature made in the image of God can look at the sky and the world around him, and see that God is who He says He is,

> *for that which is known about God is evident to them and made plain in their inner consciousness, because God Himself has shown it to them. For ever since the creation of the world His invisible nature and attributes, that is, His eternal power and divinity, have been made intelligible and clearly discernible in and through the things that have been made–His handiworks. So men are without excuse–altogether without any defense or justification. (Rom. 1:19-20)*

There's no excuse for any man who says there is not a God. The rabbis have put an interesting law in the Talmud, saying that God even accepts the sacrifice of a heathen bringing his worship to an idol, because in reality, he's seeking the living God. Since nobody has spoken to him about the living God, all he knows is the idol made by his father's hands. He brings a gift to the idol because he knows no better. The rabbis say that God looks at this with favor because the man is truly, in his heart, seeking the living God. This is why Jesus commanded you and me, "Go out, and make disciples of men. Go tell that heathen idol worshiper who I really am."

> *Behold, I am about to make Jerusalem a cup or a bowl of reeling to all the peoples round about, and against and upon Judah also it will be in the siege against Jerusalem. (Zech. 12:2)*

We don't know how soon there will be a siege taking place against Jerusalem, but all signs are pointing to it.

> *And in that day, I will make Jerusalem a burdensome stone for all peoples; all who lift it or burden themselves with it shall be sorely wounded. And all the nations of the earth shall come and gather together against it. (Zech. 12:3)*

In the end times, when all nations gather against Jerusalem in the final battle, and Christ is on His way back, the Body of believers will have been taken up already. The Rapture will have taken place. How else would God be able to get the United States to take a position against Israel?

> *In that day, says, the Lord, I will smite every horse of the armies that contend against Jerusalem with terror and panic, and his rider with madness; and I will open My eyes and regard with favor the house of Judah, and I will smite every horse of the opposing nations with blindness. And the chiefs of Judah shall say in their heart, The inhabitants of Jerusalem are my strength in the Lord of hosts their God.*
>
> *In that day will I make the chiefs of Judah like a big, blazing pot among sticks of wood, and like a flaming torch among sheaves of grain; and they shall devour all the peoples round about, on the*

right hand and on the left. And they of Jerusalem shall yet again
dwell and sit securely in their own place in Jerusalem. And the
Lord shall save and give victory to the tents of Judah first, that the
glory of the house of David and the glory of the inhabitants of
Jerusalem may not be magnified and exalted above Judah. And in
that day will the Lord guard and defend the inhabitants of
Jerusalem; and he who is spiritually feeble and stumbles among
them in that day of persecution shall become strong and noble like
David; and the house of David shall maintain its supremacy like
God, like the Angel of the Lord–Jesus Christ Himself–Who is be-
fore them.
 And it shall be in that day, that I will make it My aim to de-
stroy all the nations that come against Jerusalem. (Zech. 12:4-9)

If the Body of believers have been taken up, only non-
believers will be left in the world. The Holy Spirit will have
been removed from the earth. Those left on earth will be
those who are rebellious, those who refuse to repent, those
who will be left with 12,000 witnesses of each of the tribes of
Israel to witness to them. There's only one way they can be
saved, and that is by dying for their faith like Christ died for
them.

 I will pour out upon the house of David and upon the inhabitants
of Jerusalem the Spirit of grace or unmerited favor, and supplica-
tion. And they shall look earnestly upon Me Whom they have
pierced. (Zech. 12:10a)

The Lord is speaking in the first person, letting us know
who went to the cross for us.

 And they shall mourn for Him as one mourns for his only son, and
they shall be in bitterness for Him as one Who is in bitterness for
his first-born. (Zech. 12:10b)

The people will mourn as if to say, "We never realized
that it was You, our God, our Jesus, who went to the cross for
us."

Lo, He is coming with the clouds, and every eye will see Him, even those who pierced Him; and all the tribes of the earth shall gaze upon Him and beat their breasts and mourn and lament over Him. Even so must it be. Amen—so be it. (Rev. 1:7)

In that day shall there be a great mourning in Jerusalem, as the mourning of the city of Hadadrimmon in the valley of Megiddo over beloved King Josiah, who was mortally wounded at thirty-nine, and for whom the people's grief was extraordinarily deep. Like that will be the mourning of Israel, when they recognize as their once crucified Messiah Him Who has come to reign. (Zech. 12:11)

Jesus will come to reign in the way that Israel expected Him to come the first time, not as the suffering servant, but as a King in victory and in glory.

So the land shall mourn, every family apart: the kingly family of the house of David apart, and their wives apart; the family of the house of Nathan, David's son, apart, and their wives apart; the priestly family of the house of Levi apart, and their wives apart; the family of Shimei, the grandson of Levi, apart, and their wives apart; all the families that are left, each by itself, and their wives by themselves, each with an overwhelming individual sorrow over having blindly rejected their unrecognized Messiah, Jesus Christ. (Zech. 12:12-14)

There will be mourning everywhere because the people will realize their sin in rejecting Jesus Christ when He took on human flesh. He humbled Himself, He lowered Himself, and He went to the cross for us, to bear our sin and transgression and iniquity. Here in the Old Testament, God revealed Himself, saying, "The day is coming when the people will know that I, went to the cross as God the Son. He and I are One, just as Jesus said when He told Philip, 'He who has seen me has seen the Father.'"

Jesus also prayed, "I pray Father, that as You are in Me, that We will be in them, that as You and I are One, We will be one together."

We cannot separate God and Jesus. They are One. We cannot end up with three different personalities, Father, Son, and Holy Spirit. The Godhead is One. In the Bible, you won't see any such word as trinity. It's a word the church has coined, to try to explain what it finds in the New Testament.

The New Testament tells us we are to baptize, in the *name* of God the Father, God the Son, and God the Holy Spirit. The *name is* Jesus. And that's how Peter baptized—in the name of the Lord Jesus Christ. That name includes all that God is.

There was a revelation of God in the Old Testament as God the Father. And Jesus comes as God the Son. And Jesus sends the Holy Spirit—who is still God. God is Three in One.

The trinity is a very hard thing for us to understand. But if we could understand the things of God completely, our minds would become God to us. And our minds can never save us. It's better to accept by faith and not lean to our own understanding.

While the mourning is going on, the Lord makes a promise,

> *In that day there shall be a fountain opened for the house of David and for the inhabitants of Jerusalem to cleanse them from their sin and uncleanness. (Zech. 13:1)*

There is still hope. The Lord says He will open that fountain of living water, Jesus, to cleanse them from their sin.

> *And in that day, says the Lord of hosts, I will cut off the names of the idols from the land, and they shall no more be remembered; and also I will remove from the land the false prophets and the unclean spirit. (Zech. 13:2)*

The Lord will cut off the idols, He will come against the adversary Himself. The unclean spirit of Satan will be removed as Christ comes back. Jesus Christ defeated Satan upon the cross, and now Satan is going to be tied and gagged and bound for the next thousand years (Rev. 20:1-3). He won't be able to attack God's people during that time.

> *And if any one again appears falsely as a prophet, then his father and his mother who bore him shall say to him, You shall not live, for you speak lies in the name of the Lord; and his father and his mother who bore him shall thrust him through when he prophesies. (Zech. 13:3)*

The Lord says there's only one final revelation, and that's Jesus Christ. There'll be no other prophecies given from that point on except Jesus Himself.

> *And in that day, the false prophets shall every one be ashamed of his vision when he prophesies. Nor will he wear a hairy or rough garment to deceive. (Zech. 13:4)*

The false prophets will no longer want to come back like Elijah and John the Baptist, wearing a hairy or a rough garment to deceive people, saying, "I am the one who is preparing the way of the Lord as stated in the Book of Malachi 4:5." They will know the Lord has already come.

> *But he will deny his identity and say, I'm no prophet, I am a tiller of the ground, for I have been made a bond servant from my youth. And one shall say to Him, to Jesus in His Second Coming, What are these wounds on Your breast and between Your hands?*
>
> *Then He will answer, Those with which I was wounded when disciplined in the house of My loving friends. (Zech. 13:5-6)*

Jesus Christ will say, "I came once before, and I was disciplined." He will be able to answer them by quoting from the twenty-second psalm which was written a thousand years before the coming of Christ by His ancestor David himself. "The dogs of the heathen have compassed Me round about. They have pierced My hands and My feet, and they have cast lots for My garments."

> *Awake, O sword, against My shepherd, and against the man who is My associate, says the Lord of hosts; smite the shepherd, and the sheep of the flock shall be scattered; and I will turn back My hand and stretch it out again upon the little ones of the flock. (Zech. 13:7)*

Jesus spoke about the same thing:

> *Then Jesus said to them, You will all be offended and stumble and fall away because of Me this night—distrusting and deserting Me; for it is written, I will strike the Shepherd, and the sheep of the flock will be scattered. But after I am raised up to life again, I will go ahead of you to Galilee. (Matt. 26:31-32)*

Jesus' first coming and His second coming were promised in the Old Testament. At His first coming, the Lord was disciplined. At His second coming, men will ask Him, "What is it You have in Your breast, and what are those wounds in Your hands?" And Jesus will answer, "That's what I received from My loving friends. I got that as a gift, as I went willingly to the cross for mankind, and I bore their sins, their transgressions, their iniquities. The chastisement necessary for their peace was upon Me, and by my stripes they have been healed in every area of their lives—spiritually, physically, mentally, and financially. And if you want to receive it this very day, just lift up your hand and touch the hem of My garment. It's already been accomplished. I have finished it."

> *And in all the land, says the Lord, two thirds shall be cut off and perish, but one third shall be left alive. And I will bring the third part through the fire, and will refine them as silver is refined, and will test them as gold is tested. They will call on My name, and I will hear and answer them. And I will say, It is My people; and they will say, The Lord Jesus Christ is my God. (Zech. 13:8-9)*

Most believers have gone through the refining fire of the Lord. Some are still going through it. We thank Him that He

loves us enough to give us this test, burning the garbage out
of our lives. He is bringing us to that point of purity where we
can be Christlike so that all who see us will see Jesus. We may
be the only Bible that some people will ever read.

Unfortunately we forget that sometimes. We seem to
think we can do our own thing because He's up there, and
we're down here. We have a picture of Jesus—we have it in
Sunday school—carrying a lamb in His arms. Anything you
want to do to the gentle Shepherd is all right. He would never
chastise anyone.

I have news for you. The minute you do something
wrong, He starts convicting you by His Holy Spirit. If you
don't pay attention to the conviction of the Holy Spirit, He
goes to your wife. She comes to you and says, "Honey, I think
you're doing something which isn't kosher. You'd better
straighten yourself out, because—"

If you don't pay attention to the Holy Spirit and your
wife—they make a majority, and they're both right—then He
goes to your best friend. And your best friend comes to you
and says, "Michael, Michael, what do you think you're doing?
That's not right with the Lord."

And if you don't make it right with the Lord, then He
goes to the pastor or the elders of your fellowship. He says,
"All secret things will be brought to light," and if we don't
humble ourselves before the Lord, He does it for us. That's
the hard way.

The easy way is to go and say, "Jesus, I repent, forgive
me." When we do that, Satan is always standing there ready to
bring us under condemnation. He says, "You know that sin
you committed exactly six-and-a-half years ago at 5:55 P.M.?
On March 15? Jesus cannot possibly forgive that."

Satan always starts to bring us under condemnation. He's
the accuser. And pretty soon he's talked us into it. We place
ourselves under condemnation. But Scripture says, "There *is*
no condemnation for those who are in Christ Jesus."

When we go to Jesus and say, "Lord, forgive me of my sins which I committed yesterday," Jesus says, "What sin are you talking about? The one you confessed last night? I have already forgiven you of all your sin, and I have forgotten it. Now you forgive yourself and you forget it."

I remember the days when Betty and I used to have arguments, and I would bring things up from nineteen-and-a-half years before. I could give you the precise time—the day, the hour, the date, the minute even.

If Jesus forgave and forgot it, why am I remembering it? Because the devil is there working, and he would like to stir up trouble in our home. He knows that his time is short right now, that Jesus is on His way back. All signs are pointing to the time when Satan's going to be bound for a thousand years. Until that day, however, we have to learn how to cope with him.

I can have a glorious day of ministering all day long, and the minute I cross the threshold into my home in the evening, something happens. I lose the anointing, and I get a grouch on my face, and I say, "Honey, is supper ready?" When she says, "Well, it'll be ready in about forty-five minutes," I think I'll die if I have to wait that long.

"How come it's not ready yet?" I yell at her. And right away, I'm ready to pick a fight.

There are two ways Betty can go.

She can put her hands on her hips and say, "Well, if you'd let me know what time you're coming home instead of being the way you are—I never know when to expect you—then I'd know when to have dinner ready." If she started out like that, we'd have a grand and glorious fight, I'd probably have to go to bed hungry, and Satan would stand by and laugh himself to death, because two Christians would be fighting. This is what he wants. He's trying to break up homes in these end times.

But praise the Lord, the Lord gave my Scotch-Irish Presbyterian wife an abundance of good common sense. She prayed for me all those years, for me to come to Jesus, saying, "Lord, I don't care what You have to do to him. If You have to break every bone in his body, I want him saved." Praise God He answered her prayers. And do you know what she starts doing when I come home all out of sorts? She starts singing in the Spirit. And as she starts singing in the Spirit, I know there's not going to be a fight. Even I don't try to pick a fight with Jesus. I simply cannot do it. When Betty starts praising the Lord, Satan has to flee. Jesus promised that if we'd rebuke the devil, he'd flee from us. He'd have no choice—he'd have to run. Jesus sits enthroned on the praises of His people. He is always right in our very midst when we are praising Him. The more He refines us, the more we can praise Him and reflect His glory. *

And the Lord spoke through the prophet Zechariah, saying,

> *Behold, a day of the Lord is coming, when the spoil taken from you shall be divided among the victors in the midst of you. For I will gather all nations against Jerusalem to battle and the city shall be taken and the houses rifled, the women ravished, and half of the city will go into exile, but the rest of the people shall not be cut off from the city. (Zech. 14:1-2)*

God Himself will bring all nations against Jerusalem, He will allow the ravishing of the women, the exiling of half the people, because at this point, the people of Israel are still refusing to accept the Lord Jesus Christ as their Savior.

> *Then shall the Lord go forth and fight against those nations, as when He fought in the day of battle. (Zech. 14:3)*

The Lord Jesus Christ will go forth against those nations, and He will be exalted, lifted up, and vindicated. All the world will see Him and know He is the Messiah. The Buddhists will know, the Confucians will know, the cultists will know, even nominal Christians will know that Jesus Christ is who He says He is.

> *His feet shall stand in that day upon the Mount of Olives, which lies before Jerusalem on the east. (Zech. 14:4a)*

When you stand on the Mount of Olives, you are facing the Golden Gate. This Gate Beautiful, the eastern gate, has been sealed shut for the last 453 years. In June of 1967, as King Hussein of Jordan was about to enter triumphantly into Jerusalem, which had not been in the hands of the people of Israel for the last two thousand years, the Lord allowed war to break out to prevent that gate from being opened. The gate has remained shut; it's the very same gate through which Jesus entered triumphantly into Jerusalem once before on Palm Sunday, and it is the gate through which He will enter in once again when He returns in glory, and His feet will stand on the Mount of Olives.

> *And the Mount of Olives shall be split in two from the east to the west by a very great valley; and half of the mountain shall remove toward the north, half of it toward the south. (Zech. 14:4b)*

The Mount of Olives is splitting now, making a pathway for His feet to enter through that valley—leading from the very place where He stood when He ascended into heaven. The latest seismograph reading shows that the split in the Mount of Olives is already twenty-five feet wide. He will return to the very same spot, He will enter in once again through the Golden Gate.

> *And the Lord says, You shall flee by the valley of My mountains. (Zech. 14:5a)*

This was clearly prophesied once before by the prophet Isaiah:

> *Oh, that You would rend the heavens, and that You would come down, that the mountains might quake and flow down at Your presence, as when fire kindles the brushwood and the fire causes the waters to boil; to make Your name known to Your adversaries, that the nations may tremble at Your presence! (Isa. 64:1-2)*

All nations will have surrounded Jerusalem in the end times, all nations will be there to see Christ Jesus in full victory. There'll be nobody who can say, "I don't know who this Messiah is."

> *The valley of the mountains shall reach to Azal, and you shall flee as you fled from before the earthquake in the days of Uzziah king of Judah: and the Lord my God–Zechariah's God–shall come, and all the holy ones–saints and angels–with Him. (Zech. 14:5)*

In Matthew, we read:

> *When the Son of man comes in His glory, His majesty and splendor, and all the holy angels with Him, then He will sit on the throne of His glory. (Matt. 25:31)*

The Lord's throne is in heaven now, but when He comes down, He will sit enthroned on the praises of His people because He inhabits the praises of His people. If we're praising Him, and we are His people, we will be His throne as long as we praise Him.

We can praise Him when we have a trial, a test, a tribulation, when somebody breaks our sprinkler system. We can praise Him when the kids next door are up until one o'clock in the morning, swimming in the pool, making so much noise they keep us awake. Yes, we can praise Him always, no matter what.

And something else will happen in the end times:

> *It shall come to pass in that day that there shall not be light; the glorious and bright ones, the heavenly bodies, shall be darkened. (Zech. 14:6)*

In the beginning, when God created the heavens and the earth, darkness was on the face of the deep, but then God spoke, saying, "Let there be light," and there was light (Gen. 3.)* It was the light of Jesus Christ maintaining, sustaining, upholding the entire universe, because the sun and moon were not called into existence until the fourth day. In the same way, when Jesus comes back again, there shall not be light as we have known it,

> *But it shall be one continuous day, known to the Lord, not day and not night, but at evening time there shall be light. (Zech. 14:7)*

When Jesus Christ comes, it will be one continuous day, as it was in the very beginning when a day with the Lord was as a thousand years. This is the Millennium we're speaking about. This is the Sabbath day of rest that the Lord says He will usher in. The sixth day is just about to close, and Zechariah says that the next day shall be one continuous day, a day when at evening time there shall be light, coming from the light of the world, Jesus Christ Himself.

> *And it shall be in that day, that living waters shall go out from Jerusalem, half of them to the eastern (Dead) Sea, half of them to the western (Mediterranean) Sea; in summer and in winter shall it be. (Zech. 14:8)*

The living water is Jesus Christ Himself. Today, everything that's alive in the river Jordan, symbolic of life in Jesus Christ, dies the minute it hits the abomination of Sodom and Gomorrah, the spirit of Babylon, the Dead Sea. But in the end times, the Dead Sea and the entire area of Sodom and Gomorrah will flourish and will start to grow again.

> *And the Lord shall be King over all the earth. (Zech. 14:9a)*

---

*See the author's *Jesus in Genesis* (Plainfield, N.J.: Logos International, ©1975).

Jesus taught us to pray, "Thy kingdom come. Thy will be done in earth as it is in heaven." When the Lord is King in earth, His *will* will be done in earth as it is in heaven. We will have heaven on earth, the kingdom of God right here among us.

> *And in that day the Lord shall be one, and His name one. (Zech. 14:9b)*

The one name will be Jesus. All men will know that Jesus is the name of the Lord. The trinity will not cease. But there'll be a universal recognition of Jesus Christ as God, as Lord of lords and King of kings.

Today, people still have a tendency to separate Jesus Christ from God, but in the last days, everybody will know that in Jesus is the fullness of the Godhead bodily. He's not just a fractional one-third or something. When Jesus was here in the flesh, He glorified the Father. When He sent the Holy Spirit, the Holy Spirit glorified Jesus Christ, bringing us to conviction, lifting and exalting Christ Jesus always. And when Christ's Second Coming takes place, all people will know that He is one with the Father. The cults—Jehovah's Witnesses, Mormons, etc.—have a tendency to separate the trinity, to say that God the Father is separate from God the Son. But they can't be separated. The minute you separate them, you're worshiping three different gods, which would not be the real God. We still worship the God of Abraham, Isaac, and Jacob because we inherited the Abrahamic covenant, and we became sons of Abraham through Jesus Christ.

> *All the land shall be turned into a plain from Geba to Rimmon, the Rimmon that is south of Jerusalem. But Jerusalem shall remain lifted up on its site and dwell in its place, from Benjamin's gate to the place of the former gate, to the Corner Gate, and from the Tower of Hananeel to the king's wine presses. It shall be inhabited,*

> *for there shall be no more curse or ban of utter destruction; but Jerusalem shall dwell securely. (Zech. 14:10-11)*

Jerusalem will dwell securely for the next thousand years, because Satan will be bound. And living water will flow from Jesus Christ Himself.

In Revelation we see John saying,

> *There shall no longer exist there–in Jerusalem or in any part of the earth–anything that is accursed, detestable, foul, offensive, impure, hateful or horrible. But the throne of God and of the Lamb shall be in it–in Jerusalem–and His servants shall worship Him and pay divine honors to Him and do Him holy service. They shall see His face, and His name shall be upon their foreheads. There shall be no more night; they have no need for lamplight or sunlight, for the Lord God–Jesus Christ–will illuminate them and be their light, and they shall reign as kings forever and ever through the eternities of the eternities. (Rev. 22:3-5)*

> *And this shall be the plague wherewith the Lord will smite all the peoples that have warred against Jerusalem: their flesh shall rot away while they stand upon their feet, and their eyes shall corrode away in their sockets, and their tongue shall decay away in their mouth. And in that day there shall be a great confusion, discomfiture, and panic among them from the Lord, and they shall seize each his neighbor's hand, and the hand of the one shall be raised against the hand of the other. And Judah also shall fight at Jerusalem; and the wealth of all the nations round about shall be gathered together, gold, and silver, and apparel, in great abundance. And as that plague on men, so shall be the plague on the horse, on the mule, on the camel, on the donkey, and on all the livestock and beasts that may be in those camps. And every one that is left of all the nations that came up against Jerusalem shall even go up from year to year to worship the King, the Lord of hosts, and to keep the feast of tabernacles or booths. (Zech. 14:12-16)*

Although there will be a plague, some will survive, because Jesus shed His blood for us. In this Scripture, the Rapture has already taken place, the believers have gone up and have returned with Christ as the Saints. The feasts of Passover and Pentecost have been done away with.

The Passover symbolized the passing over of the death angel. Jesus fulfilled it, and Christians observe the Passover every time they take communion. Jesus said, "Do this in remembrance of Me—until I come back." Communion and Passover are done away with at His return. And Pentecost will also be done away with because He'll be here. The only remaining festival will be the feast of tabernacles, and everybody who remains will keep the feast.

The word "tabernacle" in the Greek and the Hebrew means "He who is with us through His Holy Spirit, He that dwells among us." The living tabernacle, Christ Jesus, will be with us, and all those who remain, who have surrounded Jerusalem, will come up and worship Him one time during the year at the festival of tabernacles as they observe the living Tabernacle of God, the true Covenant, Jesus Christ Himself.

> *And it shall be, that whoso of the families of the earth shall not go up to Jerusalem to worship the King, the Lord of hosts, upon them there shall be no rain. And if the family of Egypt do not go up to Jerusalem and present themselves, upon them there shall be no rain, but there shall be the plague with which the Lord will smite the nations that go not up to keep the feast of tabernacles. This shall be the consequent punishment of the sin of Egypt, and the consequent punishment of the sin of all the nations that do not go up to keep the feast of tabernacles.*
>
> *And in that day there shall be written upon the little bells on the horses, HOLINESS UNTO THE LORD; and the pots in the Lord's house shall be holy to the Lord like the bowls before the altar. Yes, every pot in all the houses of Jerusalem and in Judah shall be dedicated and holy to the Lord of hosts; and all who sacrifice may come and take them and boil their sacrifices in them, and traders in such wares will no longer be seen at the temple. (Zech. 14:17-21a)*

The sacrifices will be done away with, the traders will be gone from the temple. Jesus drove them out once before, when He entered into the temple and said, "You have made My house a den of thieves." In those days, the people of Israel had only one way to reconcile themselves to God after they had sinned, and that was to bring in a sin offering. But there were problems with that because you would buy a five-dollar lamb out in the market and bring the sacrifice to the priest, and the priest would say, "Just a minute, buddy."

And you'd say, "What's wrong?"

"Well, you can't use the lamb for a sacrifice because you didn't buy it from the house of the Lord."

And you'd ask him, "How much is the lamb for the sacrifice?"

He'd say, "It's ten dollars."

So you'd pull out a ten-dollar bill, and you'd say, "Here's the money for the lamb."

And he'd say, "Just a minute, buddy. You don't have temple money. You have to convert your money into temple money."

So then you'd have to come up with twenty dollars to convert into ten dollars' worth of temple money to buy a five-dollar lamb.

This is the situation that existed, and Jesus said, "You have made My house a den of thieves. You have stopped the people from bringing that which I revealed to Moses clear back in the Old Testament. Their way of reconciliation with Me was through the sacrifice of the blood of this lamb until I came into the world."

Because Jesus has come, we don't need any more sacrifices. He made us right with God forever.

> *And in that day, there shall be no more a Canaanite, that is, any godless or unclean person, whether Jew or Gentile, in the house of the Lord of hosts. (Zech. 14:21b)*

This is explained in Ephesians, where we read,

> *Therefore you are no longer outsiders–exiles, migrants and aliens, excluded from the rights of citizens; but you now share citizenship with the saints–God's own people, consecrated and set apart for Himself; and you belong to God's own household. You are built upon the foundation of the apostles and prophets with Christ Jesus Himself the chief Cornerstone. In Him the whole structure is joined, bound, welded together harmoniously; and it continues to rise, grow, increase into a holy temple in the Lord–a sanctuary dedicated, consecrated and sacred to the presence of the Lord. In Him–and in fellowship with one another–you yourselves also are being built up into this structure with the rest, to form a fixed abode, a dwelling place, of God in, by, and through the Spirit, the Holy Spirit of God. (Eph. 2:19-22)*

To the orthodox Jew, the events of the Book of Zechariah are those of the first coming of the Messiah. The people of Israel refused to believe that their Messiah could come in the form of a suffering servant. They expected Him to come in glory the first time. But they will suddenly, supernaturally know, when He comes according to Zechariah's prophecy, that this is the same Jesus who came the first time as a babe wrapped in swaddling clothes, lying in a manger.

Part III

Other Old Testament Prophets

of the Coming Kingdom

Chapter 6

Isaiah and Obadiah

Zechariah was not the only Old Testament prophet who spoke of the Coming Kingdom. Others, before and after him, delivered messages from the Lord concerning Christ's return to rule as King of kings and Lord of lords. It is not surprising to find very similar messages coming through several of the prophets, because it is the Lord who is speaking, and He doesn't contradict Himself, but affirms and reaffirms His promises.

The prophet Isaiah, who has told us so much about the first coming of the Messiah Jesus, tells us some of the things that will happen after He comes back the second time, this time not as a suffering servant but as a kingly ruler:

> *And it shall be in the day that the remnant of Israel and such as are escaped of the house of Jacob shall no more lean upon him who smote them, but they will lean upon the Lord, the Holy One of Israel, in truth. (Isa. 10:20)*

After the Second Coming of Christ, when we are with Him in the Millennium as the saints who have returned with Him (the Rapture has taken place, the Tribulation is over,

Satan has been bound to stay bound for a thousand years, Christ has come back, and we have come back with Him), the remnant will lean upon Him. They will know that He is the way, the truth, and the life, and that He's the one who set them free.

> *A remnant will return, a remnant of Jacob, to the Mighty God. For though your population, O Israel, be as the sand of the sea, only a remnant of it will return and survive. The fully completed destruction is decreed, decided upon, and it is brought to an issue. It overflows with justice and righteousness, the infliction of just punishment. (Isa. 10:21-22)*

This prophecy which is to be fulfilled during the thousand-year reign is quoted from Isaiah by the apostle Paul in his letter to the Romans:

> *And Isaiah calls out over Israel: Though the number of the sons of Israel be as the sands of the sea, only the remnant will be saved. For the Lord will execute His sentence upon the earth–He will conclude, He will close, His account with men completely and without delay–rigorously cutting it short in His justice. (Rom. 9:27-28)*

God spoke through the prophet Obadiah to show us how—and why—a part of this predicted destruction, the destruction of Esau (Edom), would be accomplished:

> *The vision of Obadiah: Thus says the Lord God concerning Edom: We have heard tidings from the Lord, and an ambassador is sent forth among the nations, saying, Arise, and let us rise up against Edom to battle! (Obad. 1)*

Edom was Esau, the brother of Jacob. The descendants of Esau and of Edom today are in Turkey, in Istanbul. There are over seven hundred mosques in Istanbul alone. Paul went as an evangelist into Asia Minor, and he preached the Gospel, but the churches set up in Asia Minor have all disappeared.

Christianity has done very little in Turkey and in Asia Minor; the Turks practically wiped out the Christian Body of believers. But now, the Lord says there will be in the end times a message, saying, "Let us rise up against Edom in battle."

> *Behold, the Lord says, I will make you small among the nations, Edom; you shall be despised exceedingly. The pride of your heart has deceived you, you dweller in the refuges of the rock whose habitation is high, who says in his heart, Who can bring me down to the ground? (Obad. 2-3)*

You, Edom, have lifted and exalted yourself up above the Lord; you're arrogant enough to say to God and the entire world, "Who can bring me down? I'm the mightiest nation on the face of the earth."

Until 1918, the Turkish Empire was large and powerful. But the Lord brought them down. Turkey sided with Germany in World War I and suffered defeat at the hands of Great Britain and France who in turn dismantled the old Ottoman empire and put much of it under protectorate. Palestine became a British protectorate which helped open the way for the establishment of political Israel.

And the Lord said to Esau, to Edom,

> *Though you mount on high as the eagle, and though you set your nest among the stars, I will bring you down from there, says the Lord. If thieves came to you, if robbers by night–how you are brought to nothing!–would they not steal only enough for themselves? If grape gatherers came to you, would they not leave some grapes for gleaning? But this was done by God, not by men. How are the things of Esau searched out! All the men of your confederacy–your allies–have brought you on your way, even to the border of Israel; the men who were at peace with you have deceived you, and have prevailed against you; they who eat your bread have laid a snare under you. And there is no understanding in Edom of it. Will not I in that day, says the Lord, destroy the wise men out of Edom, and understanding out of Mount Esau, Idumea, a mountainous region? (Obad. 4-8)*

Herod, an Idumean descendant from Esau, sought to slay the Christ child. The babies who were slain were buried in the cave next to the one where Christ Jesus was born in Bethlehem.

And the Lord said through Moses,

> *In every generation will I rise against Amalek, who was a descendant of Esau, because Esau will always rise up against the people of God. I will be the One who will put him down, because he will always seek to destroy the people of the Lord. (Exod. 17:16)*

> *And your mighty men, O Teman, shall be dismayed, to the end that every one from Mount Esau will be cut off by slaughter. (Obad. 9)*

The Lord says, "I will cut off by slaughter all those who have lived by the sword." When Isaac was old and Esau came in to receive his blessing, Isaac had already given it to Jacob. And Isaac said to Esau, "You shall serve him. You shall live by the sword, you shall die by the sword." And here the Lord says every person from Mount Esau will be cut off by slaughter because they have lived by the sword.

And the Lord said to Edom.

> *For the violence you did against your brother Jacob, shame shall cover you, and you shall be cut off for ever. (Obad. 10)*

The Lord held out salvation to the Ammonites, to the Moabites, to the descendants of Ishmael, because they were all related to Abraham. But even though Esau was related to Abraham, God said, "I will cut you off forever."

> *On the day that you stood aloof from your brother Jacob, on the day that strangers took captive his forces and carried off his wealth, and foreigners entered into his gates and cast lots for Jerusalem, you were even as one of them. You should not have gloated over your brother's day, the day when his misfortune came and he was made a stranger; you should not have rejoiced over the sons of*

Judah in the day of their ruin; you should not have spoken arrogantly in the day of their distress. You should not have entered the gate of My people in the day of their calamity and ruin; yes, you should not have looked with delight on their misery in the day of their calamity and ruin; and you should not have reached after their army and their possessions in the day of their calamity and ruin. And you should not have stood at the crossway to cut off those of Judah who escaped, and neither should you have delivered up those of Judah who remained in the day of their distress. (Obad. 11-14)

The Lord is saying to Turkey, "You should not have invited the world to come in and attack your brother Israel, you should not have gloated, you should not have rejoiced. You had no love. All you had was hate, and now I cut you off."

For the day of the Lord is near upon all the nations. As you have done, it shall be done to you; your dealing will return upon your own head. (Obad. 15)

There's another way of saying it: You're going to reap what you have sown.

For as you, Esau, have drunk upon the mountain of My holiness, desecrating it in the wild revelry of destroyers, so shall all nations drink continually, in turn, of My wrath; yes, they shall drink, they shall talk foolishly, they shall swallow down the full measure of punishment, and they shall be destroyed as though they had not been. (Obad. 16)

Esau is going to be destroyed as if he had never been.

But on Mount Zion in Jerusalem there shall be deliverance, and those who escape, and it shall be holy; and the house of Jacob shall possess their own former possessions. The house of Jacob shall be a fire and the house of Joseph a flame, but the house of Esau shall be stubble. (Obad. 17-18a)

The stubble will be devoured by the fire, but there will be

on Mount Zion in Jerusalem deliverance for those who escape, and he on Mount Zion shall be holy.

> *They shall kindle and burn them and consume them, and there shall be no survivor of the house of Esau, for the Lord has spoken it. (Obad. 18b)*

If the Lord has spoken it, it shall come to pass. And the Lord tells us what the map of Israel will be like. He tells who will take what.

> *They of the South—the Negeb Desert—shall possess Mount Esau. And they of the lowland the land of the Philistines; they shall possess the land of Ephraim, and the fields of Samaria, and Benjamin shall possess Gilead across the Jordan River. And the exiles of this host of the children of Israel who are among the Canaanites shall possess Phoenicia (Lebanon) as far as Zarephath, and the exiles of Jerusalem who are in Sepharad shall possess the cities of the South, the Negev. (Obad. 19-20)*

There are two classes of Jews, the Sephardim and the Ashkenazi. The Sephardim are those who remained in and around the Holy Land instead of going into Europe, while those who went into Europe are called Ashkenazi. And the Lord said the Sephardic Jews will be down in the Negeb desert, down in the south.

> *And deliverers shall go up on Mount Zion to rule and judge Mount Esau, and the kingdom and the kingship shall be the Lord's. (Obad. 21)*

"The kingdom and the kingship shall be the Lord's." With that good news of the Millennium, Obadiah ends his writing, perhaps to go outside and shout, "Hallelujah! Praise the Lord! The King is coming!"

One of the covenants to be fulfilled during the thousand-year reign of Jesus, is the covenant that God made with David. The Lord promised by the Holy Spirit, through the lips of Isaiah,

> *And there shall come forth a Shoot out of the stock of Jesse, David's father, and a Branch out of his roots shall grow and bear fruit. And the Spirit of the Lord shall rest upon Him, the spirit of wisdom and understanding, the spirit of counsel and might, the spirit of knowledge and reverential and obedient fear of the Lord. (Isa. 11:1-2)*

The Shoot would have the seven fold spirit of the Holy Spirit upon Him. This. was fulfilled in Jesus' first coming, and it will be fulfilled again for those who come through the Tribulation to finally accept Christ Jesus as they see Him. That one-third, that small remnant, will receive the seven fold spirit of the Holy Spirit upon them, because the Lord will bless them as they accept Him.

God has been showing His grace to His people from the beginning of time. We see that Noah found grace in the eyes of the Lord. And eight people were saved and we are all descendants from those eight people. All the way back to Noah, we were bound into an everlasting covenant. The Lord says, "I will show grace and mercy for those who love Me for a thousand generations."

> *And it shall be in that day that the Root of Jesse, Jesus Christ Himself, shall stand for an ensign, a signal to all peoples; of Him shall the nations inquire and seek knowledge, and His dwelling shall be glory, and His rest will be glorious. (Isa. 11:10)*

Jesus will be a signal to *all* people. He died for everybody. Some of us have thought that He died for just our particular denomination, but He died for the Catholic, the Presbyterian, the Baptist, the Methodist, the Jew—for everybody who would receive Him. He died for all nations, white, black, Greek, slave, purple, pink—anything you want to name. He went to the cross for the person you don't like, the person you judge and criticize. He loves them with the same everlasting love He pours out on you and me. And He wants us to stop criticizing and to love them as we love ourselves. It's a big order, and the only way we can do it is for us to be willing to let Him love them *through* us. Our own love can never be sufficient.

We will have rest in His glory, and that rest will be glorious. God did not allow the people of Israel He brought forth out of Egypt to enter into His rest, because they made the golden calf and they blasphemed against His Holy Spirit by saying, "This idol we have just made with our own hands is the god that brought us forth out of the land of Egypt." After they had done this abominable thing, the Lord said, "All of you twenty years of age and older, who were counted in the census, all 603,550 of you, will fail to enter into My rest, because you failed to believe My word. Only two of you will enter in, Caleb and Joshua, because they have a different spirit. They believed My word, and they will enter into My promised rest." The Scripture in Isaiah shows that during the Millennium, the covenant made to Israel as a nation will be fulfilled. The one-third which will accept Christ Jesus as the Savior, as the Messiah, shall enter into His glorious rest.

> *And in that day the Lord shall again lift up His hand a second time to recover–acquire and deliver–the remnant of His people which is left, from Assyria, from Lower Egypt, from Pathros, from Ethiopia, from Elam in Persia, from Shinar, from Hamath in Upper Syria, and from the countries bordering on the Mediterranean Sea. And He will raise up an ensign, a signal for the nations, and He will assemble the outcasts of Israel, and gather together the dispersed of Judah from the four corners of the earth. (Isa. 11:11-12)*

From the time of the first exile in 721 B.C., the Lord has scattered Israel to the four corners of the earth. But now, He will bring them back together.

> *The envy and the jealousy which Ephraim has brought in shall de-*
> *part, and they who vex and harass Judah from outside or inside*
> *shall be cut off; Ephraim shall not envy Judah, and Judah shall*
> *not vex and harass Ephraim. But with united forces Ephraim and*
> *Judah will swoop down upon the shoulder of the Philistine's land*
> *sloping toward the west; together they will strip the people on the*
> *east, the Arabs. They will lay their hand upon Edom and Moab,*
> *and the Ammonites shall obey them. (Isa. 11:13-14)*

The Lord also speaks through Isaiah about a very strange incident to occur in Egypt during the Millennium:

> *In that day there will be an altar unto the Lord in the midst of*
> *Egypt and a pillar to the Lord at its border. It shall be for a sign*
> *and a witness to the Lord of hosts in the land of Egypt, for they will*
> *cry to the Lord because of the oppressors and He will send them a*
> *Savior, even a mighty one, and He will deliver them. The Lord*
> *will make Himself known to Egypt. (Isa. 19:19-21a)*

The same Savior who saved you and me will be sent to Egypt to bring them to salvation. During the Millennium, the Egyptians will have a chance to accept the Lord Jesus Christ. He made himself known to us, when He was here in the flesh, and He said, "No man comes unto me unless my Father brings him unto me." During the thousand-year period when there is peace and prosperity, everything will be in order exactly as it was in the beginning, before sin and death came into the world. Satan is going to be bound and gagged for a thousand years. He is not going to be able to reach anybody during that thousand-year period. It's going to be a time of praising and worshiping the Lord. And during this time, Jesus will make Himself known to Egypt.

> *And the Egyptians will have knowledge of, become acquainted*
> *with, give heed to and cherish the Lord Jesus Christ. In that day,*
> *they will worship with sacrifice of animals and vegetable offerings,*
> *they will vow a vow unto the Lord, and they will perform it. In that*
> *day, there shall be a highway out of Egypt to Assyria, the Assyrians*

will come into Egypt, the Egyptians into Assyria, and the Egyptians will worship the Lord with the Assyrians. And in that day, Israel shall be the third with Egypt and with Assyria, in the Messianic league, the Messianic covenant, a blessing in the midst of the earth, whom the Lord of hosts has blessed, saying, Blessed be Egypt My people, and Assyria, the work of My hands, and Israel, My heritage. (Isa. 19:21b-25)

We see that there will be a united people—Egypt and Assyria, enemies of Israel, and Israel will be united in a Messianic league during the thousand-year period.

Why will there be animal sacrifices again? The Lord will allow them to bring in animal sacrifices to teach them the way, the truth, and the life. He will take them back to the Levitical period, the period of the Old Covenant, to show them the preparation of the sacrifice of Christ Jesus.

When Satan is released after the thousand years, to have one last chance before he is cast into the lake of fire forever, he will go to these people who have brought in animal sacrifices, and he will say, "This day, whom do you choose? Do you still want to bring in your own animal sacrifices, or are you willing to stand by the Body of Jesus Christ and by His shed blood, accepting the sacrifice that has already been made?"

We have professed with our lips and believed with our hearts that Jesus Christ is Lord. These people will have a chance when Jesus reveals Himself to them. This is the final conversion and deliverance of Egypt.

The redemption by grace is the same promise given to you and me. The Lord is speaking, saying,

But now, in spite of the past judgment for Israel's sin, thus says the Lord Who created you, O Jacob, and He who formed you, O Israel – (Isa. 43:1a)

The Lord is speaking to two distinct people—Jacob the liar, the conniver, the cheat, the deceiver, the opportunist—

and to Israel, the ruler with God. The Lord says, "I created you, Jacob, with a free will. You can do your own thing if you want. If you want enough rope to hang yourself, be My guest. But if you would like to be formed into a new creature, I will give you a born-again experience, and I will make you into Israel, ruler with God." And He says,

> *Fear not. I have redeemed you. I have purchased you with a price, I have bought you with My body and My blood, I have ransomed you by paying the price instead of leaving you captive. I have called ed you by your name, you are Mine. (Isa. 43:1b)*

The Lord Jesus has called each of us by name. He knows every hair upon our bald heads. And now here's the greatest promise of all:

> *When you pass through the waters, I will be with you, and through the rivers, they shall not overwhelm you; when you walk through the fire, you shall not be burned, nor scorched, nor shall the flame kindle upon you The smell of smoke will not be upon you. (Isa. 43:2)*

This is redemption by grace. And the Lord says to those during the Millennium who do not yet have incorruptible bodies, "Fear not, I am with you." And that promise applies to you and me this very day, because we have accepted Jesus Christ as our Savior.

The covenant that God made to Abraham will be fulfilled during the Millennium.

> *Wait and listen, every one who is thirsty! Come to the waters. And he who has no money, come, buy and eat! Yes, come, buy priceless spiritual wine and milk without money and without price, simply for the self-surrender that accepts the blessing! (Isa. 55:1)*

There are seventy-seven hundred promises in this Bible that belong to you as a gift. There are fifteen hundred promises in regard to healing alone. They are yours for the self-surrender that accepts the blessing by faith.

The New Testament tells us that without faith, it is impossible to please God. We receive His gifts by faith just as Abraham did. God took him up by His Holy Spirit into outer space and showed him all the stars of the universe.

He said, "Abie, do you believe, as old as you are, that I can give you an heir?"

And Abie said, "Yeah, I believe You, Lord."

He said, "Do you believe that I will multiply you as the stars of the universe that you see now?"

And Abie said, "Yeah, Lord, I believe it."

Because Abraham believed the Lord by faith, the Lord accounted it unto him for righteousness, and He called him His friend. And He said, "I will make you a father of many nations." And so he is.

So now the Lord says,

> *Why do you spend your money for that which is not bread? And why do you take your earnings and blow them away for what does not satisfy? Hearken diligently to Me, and eat what is good, and let your soul delight itself in fatness, the profuseness of spiritual joy. (Isa. 55:2)*

God says that the only way we're going to be satisfied is to eat the Word, the Living Word, which He has given us, the Word of life. Jesus says, "I am the bread of life. He that eats of Me shall never die; he shall never get hungry." And the Lord says that we should delight ourselves in the fatness of the Word, and in the profuseness of spiritual joy, peace, and mercy beyond our understanding.

And He goes on to say that if you want life, you must

> *incline your ear, submit and consent to the Divine will, and come to Me; hear, and your soul shall revive; and I will make an ever-*

> *lasting covenant or league with you, even the sure mercies—good will and compassion—promised to David. Behold, I have appointed Him, the son of David, who is the Messiah, or David as representing Him, for a witness, one who shall testify of salvation, to the nations. He will be a prince and commander to all the peoples upon the face of the earth. Behold, you, Israel, shall call nations that you know not, and nations that did not know you shall run to you because of the Lord your God, and of the Holy One of Israel, for He has glorified you. (Isa. 55:3-5)*

Perfect strangers will come to you because He, the Lord Jesus Christ, has glorified you.

> *Seek, inquire for and require the Lord while He may be found, claiming Him by necessity and by right. Call upon Him while He is near. (Isa. 55:6)*

Do we require the Lord? Many of us seem to think we don't need Him all the time, that He's somebody that you just use once in a while, when you get in real trouble. That's wrong. I know, because I had to learn it the hard way. I was so disobedient, I had to write a book called *The Phenomenon of Obedience.** I had to get clobbered on the head many times before God was able to get my attention and let me know that I did require the Lord continually. I couldn't make it one day without Him.

Do you have a need? You can claim Him by the necessity of your need. That's a promise. Why don't you already have what you need? Most Christians have not because they ask not. Jesus said, "Ask and you shall receive. Seek and you shall find. Knock and it shall be opened unto you."

One day as I was thinking about this, the Lord said, "Michael, Michael, put the first letters of those three together—ask, seek, knock. They spell a-s-k. If you ask, I will supply all of your needs according to My riches in glory."

---

*(Plainfield, N.J.: Logos International 1974)

> *Let the wicked forsake his way, and the unrighteous man his thoughts of unrighteousness; and let him return to the Lord, and He will have love, pity, and mercy for him; and to our God, for He will multiply to him His abundant pardon. (Isa. 55:7)*

Here we see grace for the sinners who repent, and the blessing of God upon them as they return to the Lord.

> *My thoughts are not your thoughts, neither are your ways My ways, says the Lord. (Isa. 55:8)*

He says, "I know you're going to try to define Me, limit Me and put Me into a little box. But guess what, people? You're in *My* little box. I'm not in your hands, but you are in My hands. Don't get hung up on whether you should do this or you should do that or you shouldn't do this or you shouldn't do that, because I fulfilled all of the law for you. The only thing I want you to remember is to love the Lord your God with all your heart, soul, and mind, and to love your neighbor as yourself. On this hangs all the law and all the prophets.

"The way I have loved you is the way I want you to love one another. I loved you to the point of death. That's the way I want you to love one another. Be willing to lay down your life for your friends.

"My ways are not your ways, so don't try to figure Me out. You can't do it. One day I will work with you one way; the next day I'll work with you another way. I don't always work with you the same way."

We've learned the truth of that at Melodyland, where we have ten thousand people worshiping with us in our three Sunday morning services. We don't print a worship bulletin with the order of worship in it, because we have learned that Jesus and His Holy Spirit never operate the same way twice. Every Sunday, every worship service, is different. The minute we think we're settling into a pattern, He changes it. As we are yielded to let Him lead us by His Spirit, He ministers to the needs of the people as we call upon Him in the language of the Holy Spirit and in song and praise and thanksgiving. We don't know what we need, but He does, and as we pray in the Spirit, He answers our needs.

> *For as the heavens are higher than the earth, so are My ways higher than your ways, and My thoughts are higher than your thoughts. For as the rain and snow come down from the heavens, and return not there again, but water the earth and make it bring forth and sprout that it may give seed to the sower and bread to the eater, so shall My word be that goes forth out of My mouth; it shall not return to Me void, without producing any kind of effect. It will not come back to Me useless, but it shall accomplish that which I please and purpose, and it shall prosper in the thing for which I sent it. (Isa. 55:9-11)*

God's Word will never come back void or empty. He sends His word with a purpose, and it always accomplishes its purpose. The Lord says some of us will plant a seed, some of us will water the seed, and some of us will harvest the crop.

I was in Pennsylvania, recently where my dear friend, Joe Garlington, teaches every week. The place was packed. I preached a single message, and four or five hundred people came forth for prayer to receive Christ and the Baptism in the Holy Spirit. It was nothing I did, it was what Jesus did. Joe Garlington planted the seed, somebody else watered that seed, and the Lord gave me the privilege of harvesting the crop for Him. I was there for only one meeting, but His Word has been going forth there every week. And the Word will never come back void or empty. It'll accomplish the purpose for which the Lord has sent it.

> *The Lord says, As the grape juice is found in the cluster, and one says, Do not destroy it, there is a blessing in it, so I will do for My servants' sakes, that I may not destroy them all. (Isa. 65:8)*

The Lord likens Israel to a cluster of grapes, out of which a small remnant will be saved, because there's still juice, there's still blessing, in it. The righteous will have an inheritance with Christ Jesus, but those who have become apostate will be destroyed. Then the Lord says,

> *I will bring forth an offspring from Jacob, and from Judah an inheritor of My mountains. My chosen and My elect shall inherit it, and My servants shall dwell there. And the plain of Sharon shall be a pasture, and a fold for flocks, and the valley of Achor a place for herds to lie down, for My people who have sought me, who have inquired of Me, who have required Me by the right of their necessity, and by the right of My invitation. (Isa. 65:9-10)*

The Lord Jesus extended an invitation to us, and the minute we accepted it and came to Him, He gave us certain rights, one of them being the right to eternal life, here for a short time, and in eternity forever. We live eighty, ninety, a hundred years on earth, and then we're with the Lord forever.

Or, you can refuse Jesus' invitation and you can have your own individual hell. Each person has his own particular hell and the Lord puts us through it if we're not right with Him.

Take flying, for instance. Flying isn't bad. But when the air starts to get turbulent, I'd rather be anywhere else other than in an airplane. I trust the Lord all the way, but I don't like the turbulence. Recently my wife and I were flying during a big storm. Hail, lightning, thunder, and wind— Then the pilot announced, as we were about to land in Pittsburgh, "It's gonna be pretty rough," and he asked all the stewardesses to sit down and fasten their seat belts.

Betty and I were sitting there, and I said, "Honey, we don't have to accept what the pilot says. We can accept what Jesus says. He gave us authority when He said, 'Where two of you are agreed as touching on any one point, that which you bind on earth, is bound in heaven.' Let's bind the effect of this turbulence on the plane." Betty agreed, and the thing was done. As we landed in the midst of that awful storm, there wasn't one bit of turbulence—even though we could hear the thunder, see the lightning, and feel the hail and the rain bombarding the plane. It was a simple matter for the Lord, very easy for Him, once He got us to agree.

> *But you who forsake the Lord, who forget and ignore My holy Mount Zion, and who prepare a table, not for Jesus Christ, but for the Babylonian god of fortune (sorcery, witchcraft, astrology, Ouija board, Tarot cards, you name it), the Lord says, If you choose that table, and if you furnish mixed drinks to the goddess of destiny, I will destine you, says the Lord, to the sword. And you shall all bow down to the slaughter, because when I called, you did not answer, when I spoke, you did not listen or obey, but you did that which was evil in My eyes, and you chose that in which I did not delight. (Isa. 65:11-12)*

This passage is talking about what will take place during the Millennium. The righteous will have an inheritance, but the apostate will be destroyed. Once again Christ will extend an invitation to those who came through the Tribulation with corruptible bodies. Those who turn back when Satan is released, to fortune, to luck, to chance, will get bound up again with Satan.

"The next Visitor to planet earth is on His way!" That's joyful news to those who love Him, to those who choose to be obedient to Him. Those who love themselves, who choose to be obedient to their own selfish desires instead of to God— they are the ones who want His coming to be delayed forever.

Chapter 7

Jeremiah and Hosea

Behold, the days come, says the Lord, that I will raise to David a righteous Branch, and He shall reign as King and do wisely, and shall execute justice and righteousness in the land. (Jer. 23:5)

Jesus will reign as King, Messiah, during the Millennium.

In His days Judah shall be saved. (Jer. 23:6a)

The salvation of Judah was not accomplished in the first coming of Christ, when He came as a suffering servant. In the Second Coming of Christ, the whole world, including Israel and Judah, will see that He is King of kings and Lord of lords.

Israel shall dwell safely: and this is His name by which He shall be called, The Lord Our Righteousness. (Jer. 23:6b)

During the Millennium, the Lord Our Righteousness will be with us, and Jerusalem will be restored under the righteous Branch who is Christ Jesus.

When we look at Israel today, we see that the ultimate uniting of the kingdom has not taken place. We see signs all over Israel, "This is under the military command of the kingdom of Judah." "This is under the military command of the kingdom of Samaria." It is still a divided kingdom. And the Lord says that during the Millennium, it will be a united kingdom. In Israel today, the inhabitants cannot agree on anything, not even on God. Everything that has happened to Israel since 1948 happened by accident and not by divine appointment, says Israel. But we know better. The Lord said in Isaiah 66:8 that as soon as Zion travailed, she would bring forth in one day that which the Lord promised. And it came to pass. Israel came forth in one day after a period of captivity and exile of twenty-six hundred years. Israel became a nation on May 14, 1948, exactly as God promised. But Israel thought it happened by accident, or that it was her own doing.

"It happened because we people of Israel are smarter than you are. And you haven't been chosen, we have. And we've got better generals than you do. We've got better thinkers than you do. We are God's chosen people, and all these things happened because God chose us to be privileged characters."

But is that what He really chose us for? No, He chose us to be missionaries; to go out and show the love of God to all people, all nations in the world, and He sent his first missionary, Abraham, into the promised land to bring forth the message that there is a God of freedom, there is a God of truth, there is a God of life, and if you choose Him, you will have life.

> *Thus says the Lord, Behold I will release from captivity the tents of Jacob, I will have mercy on His dwelling places; the city will be rebuilt on its own old mound-like site, and the palace shall be dwelt in again after its former fashion. Out of them, city and palace, shall come a new sacrifice: songs of thanksgiving and voices of those who make merry. And I will multiply them, and they shall not be few. I will also glorify them, and they shall not be small. (Jer. 30:18-19)*

The new sacrifice will be the sacrifice of lips in a song of praise and thanksgiving unto the Lord Jesus Christ. They will come to know and love Christ as we love Him.

> *Their children also shall be as in former times, and their congregation shall be established before me, and I will punish all those who oppress them. And their prince shall be one of themselves. (Jer. 30:20-21a)*

Jesus Christ will be the prince of Israel. They will know it when they see Him standing in glory on the Mount of Olives.

> *Their ruler shall come from the midst of them, and I will cause him to draw near, and he shall approach me, for who is he who would have the boldness and would dare on his own initiative to approach Me? says the Lord. When your prince approaches unto Me, then you shall be My people, and I will be your God. (Jer. 30:21b-22)*

Jesus said, "If I be lifted up, I will draw all men unto Me."

In the Millennium, the new covenant is fulfilled in the restored Israel.

> *Behold, the days are coming, says the Lord, when I will make a new covenant with the house of Israel and with the house of Judah. Not according to the covenant which I made with their fathers in the day when I took them by the hand to bring them out of the land of Egypt, My covenant which they broke although I was their Husband, says the Lord. (Jer. 31:31-32)*

The Lord was the husband of Israel, but she broke the covenant, she became an adulteress, by going out and worshiping idolatry. She did this even after He had brought her up out of bondage in the land of Egypt with His own hand.

We find Israel's unfaithfulness to the Lord and the Lord's forgiveness vividly portrayed in the book of Hosea.

Hosea had a miserable life. The Lord commanded him to marry a prostitute:

> *Then said the Lord unto me, Hosea, Go again, love the same woman, Gomer, who is beloved of a paramour and is an adulteress, even as the Lord loves the children of Israel, though they turn to other gods and love cakes of raisins which are used in sacrificial feasts of idol worship. (Hos. 3:1)*

Can you imagine God coming to you and telling you to go marry a harlot? This prophet didn't rebel, as we might have done. He was obedient to the Lord. Hosea and Gomer are symbolic of the Lord and Israel. Israel has played the harlot. She has prostituted herself in turning from the living God toward every form of abomination and idolatry she could get her hands on.

When God told Hosea to go and love Gomer again, he followed God's instructions. Hosea said,

> *So I bought her for fifteen pieces of silver and a homer and a half of barley, the price of a slave in that day and age. And I said to her, You shall be betrothed unto me for many days; you shall not play the harlot or the prostitute, and you shall not belong to another man. So will I also be to you until you have proved your loyalty unto Me and our marital relationship may be resumed. (Hos. 3:2-3)*

Here the Lord is showing Israel a picture of the Millennium when she will no longer defile herself with any form of idolatry.

> *For the children of Israel shall dwell and sit deprived many days, without king or prince, without sacrifice, without any form of idolatry, without an ephod, which is a garment worn by the priests when they are seeking the divine counsel of the Lord, and even without household gods. Afterward shall the children of Israel return, and seek the Lord their God inquiring and requiring of Him, and from the line of David, their King of kings; and they shall come in anxious fear to the Lord and to His goodness, and to His good things in the latter days. (Hos. 3:4-5)*

Hosea's picture of those latter days makes them sound absolutely perfect:

> *And in that day will I make a covenant for Israel with the living creatures of the open country, and with the birds of the heavens, and with the creeping things of the ground. I will break the bow and the sword and abolish battle equipment and conflict out of the land, and will make you lie down safely. I will betroth you to Me forever. Yes, I will betroth you to Me in perfect righteousness and justice, and in steadfast love, and in My sure mercies. I will even betroth you to Me in perfect stability, and in perfect faithfulness, and you shall know—recognize, be acquainted with, appreciate, give heed to and cherish—the Lord Jesus Christ. And in that day, I will respond, says the Lord. I will respond to the heavens . . . And they shall respond to the earth . . . and the earth shall respond to the grain and the wine and the oil . . . and these shall respond to the restored Israel who prays for a supply of them. And I will sow her for myself, I will plant her for Myself, anew in the land and I will have pity, mercy and love for her who had not obtained pity, mercy and love, and I will say to those who were not My people, You are My people, and they shall say, You are my God! (Hos. 2:18-23)*

Despite what Israel has done, in the day of the Millennium, the Lord will bring to pass the new covenant in the restored Israel. All the blessings He promised Israel, even though she had not deserved them, He will give her abundantly.

> *But this shall be the covenant that I will make with the house of Israel. After those days, says the Lord, I will put My Scripture within them, and on their hearts will I write it. I will be their God, and they shall be My people. (Jer. 31:33)*

After the days we have spoken about, the days of the taking up of the Body of believers, after the Tribulation, the Lord is going to put His Law inside us. It's not going to be just head knowledge, it's going to be a heart knowledge.

God's finger wrote the Law on tables of stone when He

gave it to Moses. But now by His finger, and with His Holy Spirit, He's going to write His Law on the hearts of flesh of those who accept Christ.

> *And they shall no more teach each man his neighbor and each man his brother, saying, Know the Lord, for they shall all know Me—recognize, understand, and be acquainted with Me—from the least of them to the greatest, says the Lord; for I will forgive their iniquity, and I will seriously remember their sin no more. (Jer. 31:34)*

In the age of the Gentile, we have gone about preaching the Gospel to fulfill the Great Commission that Jesus gave us: "Go ye out into all the world, even into Samaria, and be witnesses for Me. Make disciples of men." But during the Millennium, Christ Jesus says that we shall no more have to teach each man his neighbor and each man his brother to know the Lord, because they will know Him. He'll be there with us, and we'll know Him personally.

The Lord doesn't want any of His creation to be lost. He wants them all to be saved. But He didn't make us like puppets, He gave us free will and free choice. As free moral agents, we can rebel, or we can be obedient.

When we choose to rebel, Satan comes over and says, "Why don't you go out and commit just a little sin? It's not that big. Tomorrow you can repent of it."

When you give in to Satan, even a little bit, you let him get a hold on you! And you learn right away that sin is bondage. One sin leads to another sin, and the first thing you know, Satan has stolen you away from Jesus. The Scripture says that in the end times, even the very elect of God can be deceived. Satan is going to be trying awfully hard to steal you away. But he can't reach you if you stay on guard and remain in the Word, Who is Jesus.

The Lord had said that He would remove Jerusalem from before His face on account of their wickedness:

> *I will remove it from before My face because of all the evil of the children of Israel, and the children of Judah, which they have done to provoke Me to anger, they, their kings, their princes, their priests, their prophets, the men of Judah, and the inhabitants of Jerusalem. And they have turned their back to Me, and not their face, though I havve taught them persistently, yet they have not listened to receive instruction. (Jer. 32:31b-33)*

The message to Israel has always been the same, the message to the Christian has always been the same: From the beginning of time, after the first man's fall, when rebellion and sin came into the world, God has been saying, "Come back to Me, and you'll find life," but they have refused to listen. Furthermore,

> *they have set their abominations of idol worship in the house which is called by My name, to defile it. And they build the high places for worship of Baal in the valley of Hinnom; they have caused their sons and their daughters to pass through the fire, in worship also of the fire gods Molech and Chemosh. (Jer. 32:34-35a)*

Would you as a mother or a father take your child and sacrifice him alive to a fire god? Yet the people of Israel did this. The Lord had commanded them to drive out all those nations from before them, but they were disobedient, and as a result, they had picked up the abominable practices of the heathen round about them. And yet, the Lord said He would forgive them:

> *I did not command them, nor did it ever come into My mind that they should do this abomination, to cause Judah to sin. And now therefore, says the Lord God of Israel, concerning this city, of which you say, It shall be delivered into the hand of the king of Babylon, by sword, by famine, and by pestilence:*
>
> *Behold I will gather them, all these people, out of the countries to which I drove them in My great anger, in My wrath and in great indignation; I will bring them back to this place, and I will make them to dwell safely. They shall be My people, and I will be their God. And I will give them one heart and one way–the one*

> *heart will say "Jesus," and the one way will be Jesus—that they may reverently see Me, respect Me, obey Me, and most of all, fear Me for the good of themselves and their children after them.*
> *And I will make an everlasting covenant with them, that I will not turn away from following them to do them good. I will put My reverential fear in their hearts, that they shall not depart from Me. (Jer. 32:35b-40)*

Praise God that He feels that way about us, that He loves us so much that when we get out in left field, He's going to come out after us and bring us back in.

> *Yes, I, the Lord your God, will rejoice over them to do them good, and I will plant them in this land assuredly and in truth with My whole heart and with My whole being. For thus says the Lord: Like as I have brought all this great evil upon this people, so will I bring upon them all the good that I have promised them. (Jer. 32:41-42)*

When God permits evil to come upon us, He uses it to bring us to our full maturity. He is developing us, refining us, testing us, bringing us to the point where we can say, "Yes, Lord, I will praise You in each and in every circumstance. I will give You thanks because I know that You are my Lord and my Savior, and that You are working all things together for my good because I love You."

This is an important truth, that no matter how dark and gloomy and bad things may seem right now, in the end, it's going to be great. It's going to be fantastic, so fantastic that, like James, we can consider it joyful when we have to face trials because we know God is permitting them in order to bring us to full maturity. Hallelujah!

But during the period of the Millennium, there will not be judgment upon any, because Satan will be bound.

All the good that God promised to Israel will come to Israel in the Millennium. In the meantime, He brought evil upon Israel. Now we would like to think that it was Satan who brought the evil upon them, but it wasn't. God's own righteous judgment brought evil upon Israel—because He loved them and had to straighten them out. They had been disobedient. They had failed to trust Him, failed to believe Him.

But as He brought evil upon them, when they are obedient to receive Jesus, He brings great good upon them. He heals them in every area of their lives—spiritual, physical, financial, emotional, mental— He finished all the work that He came to do for us. He even went down into hell for us that we might not go to hell. He gave us a completed work, peace that passes all understanding, because He took the chastisement necessary for that peace. The stripes He bore for our sake correspond to the major illnesses that can kill mankind. By His stripes, we have been healed. It's done. All we need to do is believe it and receive it.

> *And fields shall be bought in this land of which you say, It is desolate, without man or beast; it is given into the hands of the Babylonians. (Jer. 32:43)*

Babylon represents the commercial system that came into existence right after the flood. After Noah found grace in the eyes of the Lord, Satan came back and started attacking man once again. The great harlot of Babylon that will be destroyed in the end times, when Jesus comes back, is the commercial enterprise which all the world has sold out to. We are hung up on commercialism, money, prosperity, the security of our nation. We think we are secure in our arms, munitions, in our armed forces, in our planes. But are we secure in the Lord?

The Lord says, "I want you to be secure in Me. I want you to put your trust and your refuge in Me, not in anything else. The minute you place it in something else, you have put another god before Me. And I am the Lord thy God. You shall have no other bombs, no other airplanes, no other jets, no other tanks before Me. I'm your bomb, I'm your jet, I'm your tank, I'm your armed forces, I'm your financial resources, I'm your everything. Why look elsewhere? All you have to do is look up and touch the hem of My garment and you'll have all you need. Ask for it, and I'll give it to you. It's as simple as that."

I praise God for the simplicity of Jesus Christ. Until you have lived under the 613 laws as I did as a Jewish rabbi, you really don't know what you're free from. As a rabbi, when I got up in the morning, I would have to say, "I thank You, Lord, for restoring my soul unto me in perfect peace which I submitted unto You last night when I went to sleep." The second prayer was, "Thank You, Lord, for not making me a woman." The third prayer was, "I thank You, Lord, for not making me a Gentile." The fourth prayer was, "I thank You, Lord, for not making me a slave."

There was no end to the rules I had to live by, but the minute I came to Jesus, I became equal with everybody. In Him there's no Greek, there's no Jew, there's no Gentile, there's no black, there's no white, there's no free, there's no slave, there's no male or female. We're all freed in Him, because He is the Truth, and the Truth has set us free. We are to remain free, and not go back into the slavery of this world.

> *Men shall buy fields for money and sign deeds, seal them and call witnesses, in the land of Benjamin, in the places about Jerusalem, in the cities of Judah, in the cities of the hill country, in the cities of the lowland, and in the cities of the South; for I will cause them to be released from their exile, from their sin, from their bondage, says the Lord. (Jer. 32:44)*

What loving forgiveness He shows to all of us!

Hosea prophesied about this same promised restoration of Israel:

> *Yet the number of the children of Israel shall be as the sand of the sea, which cannot be measured or numbered; and instead of its being said to them, You are not My people, it shall be said to them, You are the Sons of the Living God! Then shall the children of*

Judah and the children of Israel be gathered together and appoint themselves one head; and they shall go up out of the land, for great shall be the day of Jezreel for the spiritually reborn Israel, a divine offspring, the people whom the Lord has blessed. (Hos. 1:10-11)

Thus says the Lord: If you can break My covenant of the day, and My covenant of the night, so that there should not be day and night in their season; then may also My covenant be broken with David My servant, so that he shall not have a son to reign upon his throne, and my covenant will be broken also with the Levites the priests, My ministers. As the host of the stars of the heavens cannot be numbered, nor the sand of the sea be measured, so will I multiply the offspring of the son of David My servant, and the Levites who minister to Me.

Moreover, the word of the Lord came to Jeremiah, saying, Have you not noticed what these people, the Jews, are saying, The Lord has cast off the two families, Israel and Judah, which He had chosen? Thus My people have despised themselves in relation to God as His people so that they are no more a nation in their own sight. (Jer. 33:20-24)

In their own sight, Israel and Judah have not believed they are a nation. They have despised themselves in their relationship to God as His covenant people.

Thus says the Lord: If My covenant of day and night does not stand, and if I have not appointed the ordinances of the heavens and the earth, the whole order of nature, then will I also cast away the descendants of Jacob and David My servant and will not choose one of his offspring to be ruler over the descendants of Abraham, Isaac and Jacob. For I will cause their captivity to be reversed, and I will have mercy, kindness, and steadfast love for them forever. (Jer. 33:25-26)

The covenant God made with Abraham and the covenant He made with David will stand forever because they do not depend upon man's faithfulness to God but upon the faithfulness of God Himself. And the final question to be asked is not how we have lived or what work we have done, but is our name written in the Lamb's Book of Life? And praise God, it is!

Chapter 8

Ezekiel

In Ezekiel, we see the new heart and the Holy Spirit being given to Israel as a nation during the period of the Millennium.

> *And when they return there they shall take away from it all traces of its detestable things and all its abominations—sex impurities and heathen religious practices. And I will give them one heart—a heart centered on Christ Jesus—and I will put a new spirit within them, My Holy Spirit, saith the Lord. And I will take the stony, unnaturally hardened, heart out of their flesh, and will give them a heart of flesh which is sensitive and responsive to the touch and the leading of the Holy Spirit of their God That they may walk in My statutes, and keep My ordinances, and do them. And they shall be My people, and I will be their God. (Ezek 11:18-20)*

Praise God that He says it over and over again, and He doesn't give up on us. I thank Him for not giving up on me.

The Lord says that because Israel's former shepherds had not taken good care of them, He Himself, the Messiah, will be the New Shepherd.

> *Therefore will I rescue My flock, and they shall no more be a prey; and I will judge between sheep and sheep. And I will raise up over*

> *them one Shepherd, and He shall feed them, even My servant the
> son of David; He shall feed them, and He shall be their Shepherd.
> And I the Lord will be their God, and My Servant, the son of
> David, a prince among them; I the Lord have spoken it. (Ezek.
> 34:22-24)*

The Son of David, Christ Jesus, will be revealed to the
people of Israel as the Savior of the world. This has not yet
happened. The Lord has been gracious enough to lift the veil
off the eyes of some of us, so that we have seen that Jesus is
our Messiah and Savior. But the final restoration of Israel,
when all Jews see that Christ is the true Savior of the world,
will not be accomplished until the Millennium. Then, the
Lord says,

> *I will grant Israel a new covenant, a covenant of peace. I will
> cause the evil beasts to cease out of the land, and My people shall
> dwell safely in the wilderness, in the desert, and in the pasture
> land, and they will sleep confidently in the woods. And I will make
> them and the places round about My hill a blessing; and I will
> cause the showers to come down in their due season; there shall be
> showers of blessing, of good insured by God's favor. (Ezek.
> 34:25-26)*

There's the greatest insurance policy in the universe. No
matter what happens in the meantime, the Lord says that in
the end there shall be showers of blessing insured by God's
favor.

> *And the tree of the field shall yield its fruit, and the earth shall
> yield its increase, and My people shall be secure in their land; and
> they shall be confident and know, understand, and realize that I
> am the Lord—Jesus Christ—when I have broken the bars of their
> yoke, and have delivered them out of the hand of those who made
> slaves of them. And they shall no more be a prey to the nations, nor
> shall the beasts of the earth devour them; but they shall dwell
> safely, and none shall make them afraid in the day of the Messiah's
> reign. (Ezek. 34:27-28)*

The Messiah will reign during the Millennium as the King of peace. Right now, He is the Prince of peace who came to the earth in the flesh. But there is not peace on the face of this earth, and Jesus said there would not be peace at His first coming. He said, "I did not come to bring peace but a sword." When He comes back again, He will come as the *King* of peace, and we will see peace. This is a covenant of God with Israel and the entire world.

> *And I will raise up for them a planting of crops for renown, and they shall be no more consumed with hunger in the land, nor bear the reproach of the nations any longer. (Ezek. 34:29)*

Did you ever wonder where anti-Semitism came from? It came from God Himself. He said, "My people Israel, I have spoken to you for thousands of years, and you have not listened to Me. I have put you across My knees, and I have paddled you. I have used the belt, and I have used the big stick over your head, but you still won't listen. You leave Me no choice. I will have to put you in exile, and make you a reproach among nations."

In Hebrew, the word "reproach" means all who see you will turn away from you, and they'll say, "Look at that no-good Jew. That's a person of God?" But now God promises that that reproach will be taken off. And that promise was fulfilled in the miracle that took place in one day, one May 14, 1948, when Israel became a nation again after twenty-six hundred years of exile and captivity. Their reproach was gone.

> *Then they shall know positively that I, the Lord their God, am with them, and that they, the house of Israel, are My people, says the Lord God; and that you, My sheep, the sheep of My pasture, are only men, and I am your God, says the Lord God. (Ezek. 34:30-31)*

God is going to remind us once again, during the Millennium when we are with Christ Jesus, that we are nothing but men. He warns us, "Don't let it go to your big fat Jewish head that you're better than somebody else. You're still only men."

The Messiah Himself will be restoring Israel, regathering them from all nations.

> *Therefore, Ezekiel, say to the house of Israel, Thus says the Lord God· I do not do this for your sakes, O house of Israel, but for My holy name's sake, Jesus the Christ. You have profaned His Name among the nations to which you went. And I will vindicate the holiness of My great name and separate it for its holy purpose from all that defiles. My name, which has been profaned among the nations, which you have profaned among them; and the nations will know, understand, and realize that I am the Lord, the Sovereign Ruler, calling forth loyalty and obedient service, when I shall be set apart by you and My holiness vindicated in you before their eyes and yours. For I will take you from among the nations, and gather you out of all countries, and bring you into your own land. (Ezek. 36:22-24)*

We see this happening today; the Lord is bringing His people together, not only the Jews into the Holy Land, but all believers everywhere into one Body.

> *Then I will sprinkle clean water upon you, and you shall be clean from all your uncleanness, and from all your idols will I cleanse you. A new heart will I give you, and a new spirit will I put within you. I will take away the stony heart out of your flesh and give you a heart of flesh. And I will put My Spirit within you. (Ezek. 36:25-27a)*

We will be made right with Him in spite of ourselves. We will even be given new hearts, hearts of flesh upon which God will pour out His Spirit.

We know that God has already begun to fulfill His promise that He spoke through the prophet Joel that in the latter days He would pour out His Spirit upon all flesh. It began on Pentecost, but this outpouring has not yet been given to Israel as a nation, only to certain individuals of Israel. During the period of the Millennium, however, He will pour out His Spirit on that one-third as they seek Christ Jesus on the Mount of Olives. The two-thirds who reject Him will be cast away, but the one-third who accept Him as the Lord will be given new hearts, they will be sprinkled with clean water, they will have God's Spirit put within them as a nation.

> *I will cause you to walk in My statutes and you shall heed My ordinances and do them. And you shall dwell in the land that I gave to your fathers, and you shall be My people, and I will be your God. (Ezek. 36:27b-28)*

Notice the same message over and over again, God saying, "I will be your God and you shall be My people. I'm going to save you in spite of yourselves."

Praise God that He chases us. "Surely goodness and mercy will chase me all the days of my life, and I will dwell in the house of the Lord forever"—that's the literal translation of Psalm 23:6. His goodness and mercy will not merely follow me, but will chase after me, actually pursue me if I try to get away from Him. The Hound of heaven is after us all. Praise the Lord.

> *I will also save you from all your uncleannesses, and I will call forth the grain and make it abundant and lay no famine on you. I will multiply the fruit of the tree and the increase of the field, that you may no more suffer the reproach and disgrace of famine among the nations. Then you shall earnestly remember your own evil ways and your doings which were not good, and you shall loathe yourselves in your own sight for your iniquities and for your abominable deeds. Not for your sake do I do this, says the Lord God; let that be known unto you. Be ashamed and be confounded for your own wicked ways, O house of Israel! Thus says the Lord God: In the day that I cleanse you from all your iniquities I will also cause Israel's cities to be inhabited, and the waste places shall be rebuilt. (Ezek. 36:29-33)*

The Lord says that we who come back with Him with the saints in His Second Coming after the Rapture, will have our

memory banks intact. We will know what Christ Jesus did for
us so we can praise Him for the next thousand years and
thank Him that we have glorified bodies like His.

> *The word of the Lord came to Ezekiel and He said: Son of man,*
> *take a stick and write on it, For Judah and the children of Israel*
> *his companions; then take another stick and write upon it, For*
> *Joseph, the stick of Ephraim, and all the house of Israel his com-*
> *panions. (Ezek. 37:15-16)*

Today, Israel is still a divided kingdom; it is under the
military command of the kingdom of Samaria and the kingdom of Judah. There are still the same factions in Israel today
that were there in the time of Christ. The situation has not
changed, and it will not change until after the Body of believers is taken up in the Rapture, until the Second Coming of
Christ when we enter into the Millennium where the King of
peace, Christ Jesus, will reign with us and we will reign with
Him.

The Lord is giving Ezekiel a picture prophecy which will
come to pass at a later time. He tells Ezekiel to take those two
sticks,

> *and join them together into one stick that they may become one in*
> *your hand. And when your people say to you, Will you not show us*
> *what you mean by these? Say to them, Thus saith the Lord God of*
> *Israel: Behold, I will take the stick of Joseph, which is in the hand*
> *of Ephraim, and the tribes of Israel his associates, and will join*
> *with it the stick of Judah, and make them one stick, and they shall*
> *be one in My hand. (Ezek. 37:17-19)*

When Solomon committed his abomination before the
Lord, he violated the commandment God gave in the beginning of time. God had said that a man should leave his father
and his mother and cleave unto his wife and they should become one flesh. Poor Solomon got hung up with a *thousand*
heathen wifes, and a thousand heathen abominations and

idolaties came into the house of the Lord as a result. God didn't like it at all, but He said to Solomon, "Because I made a promise to your father David, I will not permit the destruction of the kingdom until after your death. I'm not doing this for you, I'm doing it for your father David because from him is coming the Son of David, Christ Jesus, the Savior of the world."

And at the appointed time, the ten tribes of Israel under the leadership of Ephraim went up north and established the kingdom of Israel at Samaria. Two tribes remained in the south, the tribe of Judah and the tribe of Benjamin. The kingdom will remain divided until the Millennium when the Lord will take the stick of Joseph and join with it the stick of Judah and make them one stick. "They shall be one in My hand, saith the Lord. They're going to be one united kingdom in the hand of Christ Jesus during the Millennium."

> *Now when the sticks on which you write shall be in your hand before their very eyes, then say to them, Thus says the Lord God: Behold, I will take the children of Israel from among the nations to which they have gone, and I will gather them from every side and bring them into their own land. (Ezek. 37:20-21)*

This prophecy has been only partially fulfilled, because the Jews are still scattered. There are only 2.7 million Jews in the whole state of Israel. There are only 3.5 million Jews in Russia and more than 6.5 million Jews in the United States of America. However, God will bring them back, He will gather them from every side and bring them into their own land.

> *I will make of them one nation in the land, upon the mountains of Israel; one King shall be King over them all; and they shall no longer be two nations, neither be divided into two kingdoms any longer. They shall not defile themselves any more with their idols and their detestable things, or with any of their transgressions; but I will save them out of all their dwelling places, and from all their backslidings in which they have sinned, and I will cleanse them. So*

> *they shall be My people, and I will be their God. And David My*
> *Servant, the Son of David, shall be King over them, and they all*
> *shall have one Shepherd. (Ezek. 37:22-24a)*

Jesus is the Good Shepherd who laid down His life for
His sheep. In the Holy Land today, Arab shepherds lead their
sheep. The shepherd stays out in front, and the sheep follow
him. Wherever he goes, they go. And they will follow only the
voice of the shepherd that they know.

I speak Arabic fluently, and when I was in the Holy Land
recently, I went to an Arab shepherd and said, "I'll give you
a buck if you'll let me lead your sheep for a minute." He
pocketed the money, said, "Okay, be my guest."

I started calling the sheep in Arabic just like their
shepherd did. But they did not recognize my voice, and they
would not follow me. They just stood right there, stubborn as
mules. They would not follow any shepherd other than the
one whose voice they knew already.

We have heard the voice of our Good Shepherd, Jesus
Christ. And the Lord says that during the Millennium, physical Israel will know that they have one Shepherd. They will
recognize His voice. They will know that He is the Savior who
came the first time as a suffering servant, and now has come
back as the King of peace.

> *They shall also walk in My ordinances and heed My statutes and*
> *do them. (Ezek. 37:24b)*

The ordinances and the statutes are the Ten Living
Words, the decalogue which God gave us on Mount Sinai.
Four of them are statutes dealing with the vertical relationship between ourselves and God, showing us how to get along
with Him. The remaining six deal with the horizontal relationship. In the Millennium, we'll have one Shepherd, and we
will walk in the love of Jesus. He said, "If you love Me, you will
keep My commandments." And we will be keeping His com-

mandments as we walk in His ordinances and heed His statutes and do them.

> *Then they shall dwell in the land in which your father dwelt, that I gave to My servant Jacob; and they shall dwell there, they and their children and their children's children, for ever; and the Son of My Servant David shall be their Prince and their King for ever. I will make a covenant of peace with them; it shall be an everlasting covenant with them; I will give blessings to them and multiply them, and will set My sanctuary in the midst of them forever. My tabernacle also shall be there with them. (Ezek. 37:25-27a)*

Who is the tabernacle? In the Book of Revelation, John says,

> *I saw no temple in the city, for the Lord God Omnipotent Himself and the Lamb Himself are its temple. (Rev. 21:22)*

Christ Jesus is the temple, He is the tabernacle. He will be in the midst of them forevermore.

> *And I will be their God, and they shall be My people. Then the nations shall know as they see you, they will understand and realize that I the Lord do set apart and consecrate Israel for holy use, when My sanctuary shall be in their midst for evermore. (Ezek. 37:27b-28)*

Praise God that He insists on being our God and upon our being His people in spite of ourselves. Most of us are going to try to get away into left field, but He's not going to let us. He went to the cross and died for us. He paid a price. He bought us with His body and His blood, and He's going to save us in spite of ourselves. I praise God that He loved me enough that while I was still an arrogant Jewish rabbi, He thought enough of me to reveal Himself to me and say, "Michael, Michael, why do you hate Me?" And when I realized who He was and what He had done for me, I just *had* to love Him.

Chapter 9

Micah and Malachi

Micah prophesied about the restoration of Israel:

> *I will surely gather all of you, O Jacob; I will surely collect the remnant of Israel; I will bring them, Israel, together as sheep in a fold, as a flock in the midst of their pasture. They, the fold and the pasture, shall swarm with men and hum with their much noise. The breaker, the Messiah, will go up before them. They will break through; they will pass in through the gate and they will go out through it. And their King will pass on before them, the Lord at their head. (Mic. 2:12-13)*

In His Second Coming, Jesus will be right there in front of them, He will be at their head. In the Hebrew, the implication is that when God is at our head, in front of us, He is also behind us and on all sides of us. The divine protection of the Lord surrounds us by a wall of fire which nothing and nobody can penetrate. His love, His joy, and his peace truly pass all understanding.

In Micah, we find the promise of the coming kingdom of God:

> *But in the latter days, it shall come to pass, that the mountain of the house of the Lord shall be established as the highest of the*

mountains, and it shall be exalted above the hills, and peoples shall flow to it. Many nations shall come, and say, Come, let us go up to the mountain of the Lord, to the house of the God of Jacob; that He may teach us His ways and that we may walk in His paths. For the law shall go forth out of Zion, and the word of the Lord from Jerusalem. (Mic. 4:1-2)

The law will flow from Zion itself, and the word of the Lord from the Mount of Olives in Jerusalem. Jesus Himself will be the teacher on the Mount of Olives.

For the last several years, I've been taking groups of people to Israel every year. Up until three years ago, I always stayed in the city of Jerusalem, and it would be so hot there I couldn't breathe. It was nice enough outside, but in the hotel room, there was no air. And I said, "Lord, why have You been doing this to me for the last five years? You put me in the best hotel, but there's no air, and we perspire all night long, and we can't sleep."

He said to me, "Well, Michael, why don't you read your Bible? Read what I did when I was ministering around Jerusalem."

So I opened up the Gospels and read that when Jesus finished ministering in Jerusalem, He always went up to the Mount of Olives.

I went up to the Mount of Olives at four o'clock in the afternoon, and there was a beautiful breeze blowing through there, natural air-conditioning. I said, "Thank You, Lord." For the last three years, we've stayed on the Mount of Olives in the finest hotel overlooking the city of Jerusalem, the Golden Gate, and the site of the temple. We have natural air-conditioning.

He shall judge between many peoples, and shall decide for strong nations afar off; and they shall beat their swords into plowshares, and their spears into pruninghooks; nations shall not lift up sword against nation, neither shall they learn war any more. (Mic. 4:3)

When the King of peace is back, we will have a thousand years of peace with Him.

> *But they shall sit every man under his vine and under his fig tree,*
> *and none shall make them afraid; for the mouth of the Lord of*
> *hosts has spoken it. For all the the peoples now walk every one in*
> *the name of his own god, but we will walk in the name of the Lord*
> *our God for ever and ever. (Mic. 4:4-5)*

Do we Christians sometimes walk in the name of our own god? Do we always walk in the name of Jesus? Anything that comes between you and Jesus has become another god between you. It might be your husband, your wife, your children. But everything you have has been given as a trust to you from the Lord Jesus Christ. We have to release our families, our wives, our husbands, our children, unto the Lord and say, "Thank You, Jesus. I know that all things are working together for my good, that whatever circumstance I find myself in this very day is from You, and You are leading me from circumstance to circumstance to make me what You want me to be." For that, we should praise the Lord.

> *In that day, says the Lord, I will assemble the lame, I will gather*
> *those who have been driven away, and those whom I have afflicted.*
> *I will make the lame a remnant, and those who were cast off, a*
> *strong nation; and the Lord shall reign over them in Mount Zion*
> *from this time forth and for evermore. And you, O tower of the*
> *flock, the hill and stronghold of the daughter of Zion, unto you the*
> *former dominion shall come, the kingdom of the daughter of*
> *Jerusalem. (Mic. 4:6-8)*

All this will happen in the Millennium, fulfilling the covenant that God made with David.

Micah speaks also of the remnant who will be forgiven.

> *Who is a God like You, Who forgives iniquity and passes over the*
> *transgression of the remnant of His heritage? (Mic. 7:18a)*

The Lord promised that there would be a remnant of Israel that would come through the Tribulation, and He is just and faithful to forgive us of our sin, our transgression, and our iniquity. The Israelites were in Egypt when for the first time in the earth they knew that God was a God of freedom, liberty, and truth, a God who sets people free and transforms them. At Mount Sinai, all the people of Israel heard His voice with their own ears when He said, "I am the Lord thy God who brought you up out of slavery, out of bondage, out of sin."

> *He does not retain His anger for ever, because He delights in mercy and loving-kindness. He will again have compassion on us, He will again subdue and tread under foot our iniquities. (Mic. 7:18b-19a)*

Praise God, our iniquities are subdued. That means that Satan is under Jesus' foot, bound and tied and gagged for a thousand years. We can't sin even if we tried.

> *You will cast all of our sin into the depths of the sea. You will show your faithfulness and perform the sure promise that you made to Jacob, and you will show loving kindness and mercy to Abraham as You have sworn to our fathers from the days of old. (Mic. 7:19b-20)*

God is still the God of forgiveness and the God of faithfulness and love, even when we complain against Him.

In Malachi, we find an interesting dialogue between the Lord and His grumbling people:

> *Your words have been hard and strong against Me, says the Lord (Mal. 3:13a)*

God is telling Israel that they have been critical of Him. They have continually complained against Him: "So what kind of God is this that we have? Where's all that love?

Where's all that grace? Where's all that mercy that You promised us?" They forgot to count their blessings, yet if we
counted our blessings for this one day alone, we wouldn't
have enough paper to write them on.

Yet you say, What have we spoken against You? (Mal 3:13b)

And the Lord answers Israel's question, saying,

*You have said, It is useless to serve God. And what profit is it if we
keep His ordinances and walk gloomily and as if in mourning ap-
parel before the Lord of hosts? (Mal. 3:14)*

The Israelites had asked, "What profit is in it for us to
serve the living God? We haven't seen any increased prosperity come out of this situation of walking with God. Loving
Him with all our heart, and soul, and mind, and loving our
neighbor as ourself—where has it gotten us? Nowhere."

The Lord told them, "You have said this in your heart.
You have said it with your lips. You have proven it with the
way you look. You walk around as if you're dead. Your heart
ought to tell your face that you're God's special chosen
people. The world ought to be able to tell by looking at them
that My people belong to Me. They shouldn't be walking
around all frozen and cracked up. They should have a smile
upon their faces."

You should be able to tell Jesus freaks, charismaniacs,
two miles away. They walk around happy all the time, never
saying just plain, "Good morning," or "Good afternoon," or
"Good night," but saying, "Praise the Lord!" or "Thank You,
Jesus!"

In California, our teenagers can drive up to the gas sta-
tion and say, "Put in twenty-five cents worth of gas, please.
Praise the Lord! Thank You, Jesus! Hallelujah!" And before
the guy gets through putting in twenty-five cents worth of
gas, he's on his knees, accepting the Lord Jesus as his Savior.

The Lord says it's no good if you walk around gloomy, as if you have on clothes of mourning for somebody who has died. The Lord is a living Lord.

> *And now consider the proud and arrogant happy and favored; evildoers are exalted and prosper. Yes, and when they test God, they escape unpunished. (Mal. 3:15)*

Israel had its eyes and ears focused on those who sinned and apparently got by with it rather than on the goodness of God. "Look at the evildoers," they said. "The evildoers are exalted, and they prosper, and You don't punish them. How come we Christians and we people of Israel who walked in Your statutes and commandments and ordinances are having such a rough time of it?"

While some were doing all this grumbling, others feared the Lord and earned a rich reward:

> *Then those who feared the Lord talked often one to another, and the Lord listened and heard it, and a book of remembrance was written before Him of those who reverenced and worshipfully feared the Lord, and who thought on His name. (Mal. 3:16)*

Those who thought upon the wonderful name of Jesus constantly, who didn't grumble against God but worshiped and revered Him, had their names written in the book of remembrance, which is the Lamb's Book of Life for all eternity.

> *And they shall be Mine, says the Lord of hosts, in that day when I publicly recognize and openly declare them to be My jewels—My special possession, My peculiar treasure. And I will spare them, as a man spares his own son who serves him. (Mal. 3:17)*

God promises to spare those who worshipfully revere and accept Jesus Christ, whose names are in the book of remembrance. This is speaking about Israel during the Millennium. They will see Christ and a small remnant will accept

Him. When they see Christ standing on the Mount of Olives, two-thirds will still reject Him, but one-third will receive Him, receiving the way of truth and life everlasting.

> *Then shall you return, and discern between the righteous and the wicked, between him who serves God and him who does not serve Him. (Mal. 3:18)*

Israel will see the difference between the judgment handed out to the sinners and the blessings given to those who have repented and have been forgiven of sin. During the Millennium, those who fall away will fall away with Satan into everlasting damnation. Those who stand with God will inherit everlasting life.

Part IV

The New Testament Looks into

the Coming Kingdom

Chapter 10

Romans and II Corinthians

Writing to the Roman church, Paul asks a question about Israel:

> *So I ask, Have they stumbled so as to fall to their utter spiritual ruin forever, so that they can never be retrieved? By no means! But through their false step and transgression, salvation has come to the Gentiles, so as to arouse Israel to see and feel what they have forfeited in rejecting Christ Jesus, their Messiah, and so to make them jealous. (Rom. 11:11)*

Israel really is jealous. A true Israelite is the most unhappy, miserable person in the world. I can tell you from experience. If you've read *Michael, Michael, Why Do You Hate Me?* you know what a miserable existence I had. I never had love, joy, or peace. I couldn't sleep at night, I was constantly under oppression, depression, and fear. But than Jesus appeared to me and asked me, "Michael, Michael, why do you hate Me?" I fell to my knees and accepted Him as my Lord, my God, my Messiah, my Savior. And from that day, my life began to change.

I had to give up depression, oppression, fear, worrying, and sleepless nights. I had to give up all those, and in exchange, He gave me a love beyond my comprehension, a peace I still don't understand, a joy that keeps bouncing all day long. I just have to rejoice in everything. I'm so happy, I can't understand it. Jesus said, "You're not going to understand it, but I'm going to give it to you wholesale," and He did.

And I learned that I never have to worry about tomorrow, because He's already supplied all of my needs for all of my tomorrows. Jesus said, "If you commit it unto Me, it's already taken care of" so I don't worry about the next day, and I know that tomorrow's going to be even better.

Maybe you've heard the expression, "Today is the tomorrow we worried about yesterday." Ninety percent of the things people worry about never happen. But we worry anyway and that gives us ulcers, heart attacks, and cancer. When we worry and fret, we talk ourselves into the grave. We buy all of the lies of Satan. But we don't have to accept that garbage. Jesus has given us perfection and completeness. As we stand in Him, He stands in us, and greater is He who is within us than he who is out there trying to get in. He can't get in, because we're covered by the shed blood of Jesus. Satan can't come near the blood of Jesus Christ. When you start praising the Lord, the devil has to flee from you, because the Lord sits enthroned upon the praises of His people.

> *Now if their stumbling, their lapse, their transgression, has so enriched the world at large, and if Israel's failure means such riches for the Gentiles, think what an enrichment and greater advantage will follow their full reinstatement! But now I am speaking to you who are Gentiles. Inasmuch then as I am an apostle to the Gentiles, I lay great stress on my ministry and magnify my office, in the hope of making my fellow Jews jealous, in order to stir them up to imitate, copy and appropriate, and thus managing to save some of them. (Rom. 11:12-14)*

Paul really made the Jews jealous. Every time he went into a synagogue to preach the Gospel, he was eventually cast out and frequently suffered physical harm. An extra-biblical tradition has it that, when he was in Rome, they literally threw him into jail through a little hole in the ceiling onto the hard rock floor of the cave that was used for a prison. But he was not hurt. And as the jailer brought him his food every day, he heard that Jewish idiot singing, "Rejoice in the Lord always, and again I say, rejoice."

And the jailer said, "This guy is really crazy." But finally he asked the question: "Hey, Paul, what's making you so happy?"

And Paul said, "Let me tell you about Jesus. He makes me happy, gives me peace, love, and so much joy I can hardly stand it."

As Paul spoke, something began to happen in the jailer's heart, and one day that jailer lowered himself on a rope, down into the cave with Paul. There he knelt and received Jesus Christ as his Savior, too.

Paul needed some water to baptize him, and he had faith that God would supply all his needs, so he prayed, "Jesus, I need some water to baptize this guy in Your name for the remission of his sins." And out of that floor of solid rock, water flowed. Paul baptized that jailer, he put him under the water in the name of Jesus—the name of the Father, and of the Son, and of the Holy Ghost. And that jailer rose to newness of life and went out and preached the Gospel to the rest of Rome. That, according to the legend, is how the Gospel was spread there.

Paul had thought he was on his way to Spain, but Jesus had other plans for Paul, and His will was going to be done. I praise God that He did send Paul to Rome, because we have a great, beautiful body of believers in Rome and in the Catholic church today. At the Notre Dame conference last year, over 25,000 Spirit-filled Catholics heard a keynote speaker named Father Cohen. Can you imagine such a thing? The Lord is going to save us in spite of ourselves.

For if their rejection and exclusion from the benefits of salvation were overruled for the reconciliation of a world to God, what will their acceptance and admission mean? It will be nothing short of everlasting life from the dead! Now if the first handful of dough offered as the first fruits is consecrated and holy, so is the whole mass, the nation of Israel; and if the root, Abraham himself, is consecrated and holy, so are the branches which are Israel. But if some of the branches were broken off, while you, the Gentile, a wild olive shoot, were grafted in among them to share the richness of the root and sap of the olive tree, do not boast over the branches and pride yourself at their expense. If you do boast and feel superior, remember it is not you that support the Root, who is Christ Jesus, but the Root that supports you. You will say then, Branches were broken, pruned off so that I might be grafted in! That is true. But they were broken, pruned off, because of their unbelief, their lack of real faith, and you are established through faith because you do believe. So do not become proud, arrogant, conceited, but rather stand in awe and be reverently afraid. For if God did not spare the natural branches because of unbelief, neither will He spare you if you are guilty of the same offense. Then note and appreciate the gracious kindness and the severity of God; severity toward those who have fallen, but God's gracious kindness to you. That is, to you provided you continue in His grace and to abide in His kindness; otherwise you too will be cut off, pruned away. (Rom. 11:15-22)

The first fruits were Abraham, Isaac, and Jacob, representing the tithe of the people of Israel unto the Lord Jesus Christ. They were saved by faith, looking into the far distant future. Hebrews 11 is a full chapter about the Old Testament patriarchs looking into the far distant future for their salvation, hoping and trusting in the coming Messiah, Jesus Christ. Without such faith, it is impossible to please Him. He wants us to continue in His grace and to live in His kindness, to say "Praise God! I thank you for the blessings that You have shown me this very day."

And even those others, the fallen branches which are the Jews, if they do not persist in clinging to their unbelief, will be grafted in, for God has the power to graft them in again. For if you have been cut from what is by nature a wild olive tree, and against nature grafted into a cultivated olive tree, how much easier will it be to graft these natural branches back on the original parent stock of their own olive tree. Let not yourself become self-opinionated, do not become wise in your own conceits, because I do not want you to miss this hidden truth and mystery, brethren. It is a hardening insensibility that has temporarily befallen a part of Israel to last until the full number of the ingathering of the Gentiles has come in. (Rom. 11:23-25)

That ingathering of the Gentiles is almost to an end. We're seeing an overlapping right now, of Gentiles coming forth and accepting Christ Jesus as the Savior, and many Jews doing the same thing. The age of the Gentile is drawing to a close, and the age of the Jew is about to open.

And so all Israel will be saved. As it is written, The Deliverer will come from Zion, and He will banish ungodliness from Jacob. And this will be My covenant, My agreement, with them when I shall take away their sins. From the point of view of the Gospel, the good news, they, the Jews, at the present time are enemies of God, which is for your advantage and benefit. But from the point of view of God's choice—of election, of divine selection—they are still the beloved, dear to Him for the sake of their forefathers, Abraham, Isaac, and Jacob. For God's gifts and His call are irrevocable. He never withdraws them once they are given, and He does not change His mind about those to whom He gives His grace or to whom He sends His call. Just as you were once disobedient and rebellious toward God but now have obtained His mercy, through their disobedience, the disobedience of Israel, so now they also are being disobedient when you are receiving mercy, through you as messengers of the Gospel to them, which has been shown to you. Thus through the mercy which you are enjoying, they may now also receive mercy. For God has consigned, penned up, all men to disobedience, only that He may have mercy on them all alike.

O the depth of the riches and wisdom and knowledge of God! How unfathomable, inscrutable, unsearchable, are His judgments, His decisions! And how untraceable, mysterious, and undiscoverable, are His ways, His methods, His paths! For who has known

> *the mind of the Lord and who has understood His thoughts, or who has ever been His counselor? Or who has first given God anything that he might be paid back, or that he could claim a recompense? For from Him and through Him and to Him are all things. For all things originate with Him and come from Him; all things live through Him, all things center in and tend to consummate and to end in Him. To Him, be glory, and honor, and praise forever. In Jesus' name. Amen. (Rom. 11:26-36)*

The word "amen" in the Hebrew means that God our King is trustworthy. And we can all say "Amen!" to that

The covenant God made with Abraham will be fulfilled during the thousand-year reign, as will the covenant with David, the covenant with Israel as a nation, and, finally, the new covenant in regard to the nation of Israel. Paul writes about this new covenant in his second letter to the Corinthians:

> *Such is the reliance and confidence that we have through Christ toward and with reference to God. Not that we are fit or qualified or sufficient in ability of ourselves to form personal judgments or to claim or to count anything as coming from us; but our power and ability and sufficiency are from God. (II Cor. 3:4-5)*

All blessings come to us from Him. If ever we think we're doing anything for ourselves, the Lord has ways of quickly making us aware of how desperately we need Him.

> *It is He who has qualified us, making us to be fit and worthy and sufficient as ministers and dispensers of a new covenant of salvation through Christ, not ministers of the letter, that is, of the legally written code, but we are ministers of the Spirit, of God's Holy Spirit. For the code of the Law kills, but the Holy Spirit makes alive. (II Cor. 3:6)*

Each and every believer is a minister and a priest unto God. When God spoke to Israel saying, "You are a kingdom of priests," He was talking about the priesthood of all believers. As priests of God, we're to minister the new covenant and not to get hung up on the letter of the Law.

Someone told me, "My daughter has been speaking in churches, and she never wears a hat, but the Bible says that the woman has to be covered in the church. Is she displeasing God?"

Well," I said, "Paul was writing about a problem in a specific situation," and then I tried to explain to him why his daughter was on safe ground. When Paul wrote to a church in Greece saying it's not good for a woman to pray with her hair and her head uncovered, prostitutes were the only women who went around with their heads uncovered. Christian women in that place wouldn't have dreamed of going bareheaded. But we live in a land where uncovered heads do not connote wantonness among women. Thus we see that Paul was speaking to a specific situation and that his instructions do not have broad application.

And when Paul said it wasn't good for a man to have his head covered in a church, he meant that our covering, the Messiah, the Lord Jesus Christ, has already come, so we don't have to cover our own heads. Hebrews who are unbelievers cover their heads when they enter the synagogue because Jesus is not their covering. These are the things Paul was writing about, and we are foolish when we try to minister the letter and not the spirit.

On a different occasion, Paul wrote to Timothy that he should drink a little wine for his stomach's sake. In certain parts of Israel even today, the water is not purified. If you drink it as is, you'll get dysentery, but if you mix two parts of water with one part wine, the alcohol in the wine kills the bacteria, and you can drink it safely. So, Paul's words should not be taken as blanket authorization for everyone to drink alcoholic beverages. Neither do they offer much support for self-righteous abstainers.

> *Now if the ministration of the law, the dispensation of death en-graved in letters on stone, was inaugurated with such glory and splendor that the people of Israel were not able to look steadily at the face of Moses— (II Cor. 3:7)*

Moses' face had to be covered with a veil. Otherwise, those who looked upon his face would have been blinded by the brilliance and the glory of the Holy Spirit which was upon him. The glow faded and passed away, but if the giving of the law was accompanied by such glory, Paul asks, then

> *Why should not the dispensation of the Holy Spirit, that is, this spiritual ministry whose task it is to cause men to obtain and be governed by the Holy Spirit, be attended with much greater and more splendid glory? For if the service that condemns the minis-tration of doom, had glory, how infinitely more abounding in splendor and glory must be that service that makes us righteous, the ministry that produces and fosters righteous living and right standing with God! (II Cor. 3:8-9)*

Paul is writing about the ministry of the Holy Spirit. Have you noticed how the Holy Spirit operates in the matter of in-terpreting the Scriptures to us? We can read a verse of Scrip-ture from the Bible today and get one thing out of it, one specific meaning quickened to us for our need. We can read the very same verse of Scripture tomorrow and hear the Lord giving us another message through it.

> *Indeed, in view of this fact, what once had splendor, the glory of the Law in the face of Moses, has come to have no splendor at all, because of the overwhelming glory that exceeds and excels it, the glory of the Gospel in the face of Jesus Christ. For if that which was but passing and fading away came with so much splendor, how much more must that abide in glory and splendor which re-mains and is permanent!*
> *Since we have such glorious hope, such joyful and confident expectation, we speak very freely and openly and fearlessly. Nor do we act like Moses, who put a veil over his face so that the people of Israel might not gaze upon the finish of the vanishing splendor*

which had been upon it. In fact, their minds were grown hard and calloused, they had become dull and had lost the power of understanding; for until this present day, when the Old Testament, the old covenant, is being read, the same veil still lies upon the hearts of My people Israel, not being lifted to reveal that in Christ it is made void and done away with. Yes, down to this very day, whenever Moses is read, a veil lies upon their minds and hearts. But whenever a person turns in repentance to the Lord, the veil is stripped off and taken away.

Now the Lord is the Spirit, and where the Spirit of the Lord is, there is liberty, emancipation from bondage, and freedom. And all of us, as with unveiled face, because we continued to behold in the Word of God, as in a mirror, the glory of the Lord, are constantly being transfigured into His very own image in ever increasing splendor and from one degree of glory to another, for this comes from the Lord Who is the Spirit. (II Cor. 3:10-18)

Most of us seem to think that once we have our born-again experience, God has given us a diploma, and we can hang it on the wall, and say, "Praise the Lord! I have it made." But being born-again is not the end, it's just the beginning of a new life, a new life in which there is a day-by-day, minute-by-minute experience of dying out to ourselves and being transfigured, transformed, by the Spirit of the Lord into the very image of God. The Holy Spirit here is the same Holy Spirit we found in the Old Testament. He's the same Lord yesterday, today, and forever. There is no blank space between the old covenant and the new covenant. It is the same Jesus in action, the same God in operation.

Chapter 11

Galatians and Ephesians

One of the New Testament Scriptures concerning the fulfillment of God's promises to Israel during the time of the Millennium is found in Paul's letter to the Galatians.

> *All who depend on the Law, who are seeking to be justified by obedience to the Law of rituals, are under a curse and doomed to disappointment and destruction. (Gal. 3:10a)*

The law was a foreshadowing, a teacher to teach us about the coming of Christ. There was nothing wrong with the Law; it was the expression of God's holiness. But we are cursed by the Law because we are not able to live under it. We cannot possibly make it except by grace because if we break even one minor law, the Law says we've broken all of them.

> *For it is written in the Scriptures that God gave to Moses, Cursed, accursed, devoted to destruction, doomed to eternal punishment, be everyone who does not continue to abide, live, and remain, by all the precepts and commands written in the book of the Law, and practice them. Now it is evident that no person is justified, declared righteous and brought into right standing with God–through the Law. (Gal. 3:10b-11a)*

We have to be justified, because we cannot possibly make it living under the Law. We're going to break laws every minute because we're sinners. We cannot be brought into right standing with God through the Law.

> *For the Scripture says, The man in right standing with God, the just man, the righteous man, shall live by and out of faith, and he who through and by faith is declared righteous and in right standing with God shall live. (Gal. 3:11b)*

That the just shall live by faith is written back in the Old Testament in Habbakuk 2:4.

> *But the Law does not rest on faith, it does not require faith, it has nothing to do with faith, for it itself says, He who does them, the things prescribed by the Law, shall live by them, but not by faith. Christ purchased our freedom, redeeming us from the curse and the doom of the Law's condemnation, by Himself becoming a curse for us, for it is written in the Scriptures, Cursed is everyone who hangs on a tree, who is crucified, to the end that through their receiving Christ Jesus, the blessing which God promised to Abraham might come upon the Gentiles, so that we through faith might all receive the realization of the promise of the Holy Spirit.*
>
> *To speak in terms of human relations, my brethren, even if a man makes a last will and testament, a merely human covenant, no one sets it aside or makes it void or adds to it, when once it has been drawn up, signed, ratified, and confirmed. Now the promises, the covenants, the agreements, were decreed and made to Abraham and his Seed, his Offspring, his Heir. He, God, does not say, And to seeds—descendants, heirs—as if He is referring to many persons, but He said, To your Seed, your Descendant, your Heir, obviously referring to one individual who is none other than Christ, the Messiah. This is my argument: The Law, which began four hundred and thirty years after the covenant concerning the coming Messiah, does not and can not annul the covenant previously established and ratified by God, so as to abolish the promise and make it void. For if the inheritance of the promise depends on observing the Law, as these false teachers would like you to believe, it no longer depends on the promise; however, God gave it to Abraham as a free gift, solely by virtue of His promise. (Gal. 3:12-18)*

This is the way that God gives us every gift that we have, by virtue of His promise. We don't deserve it, there's no way we can earn it, but He gives it to us as a gift.

What then was the purpose of the Law? It was added—later on, after the promise, to disclose and expose to men their guilt—because of transgressions and to make men more conscious of the sinfulness of sin. (Gal. 3:19a)

If we did not receive the Law, how would we know what was right and wrong in the eyes of the Lord? And how else could we come to realize how urgent is our need for His salvation? He had to show us, and so the Law was our teacher until the coming of the Christ.

And it, the Law, was intended to be in effect until the Seed, the Descendant, the Heir, should come, concerning Whom the promise had been made. And it, the Law, was arranged and ordained and appointed through the instruments of angels, and was given by the hand of a go-between. Now a go-between has to do with and implies more than one party. There can be no mediator with just one person. Yet God is only one person, and He was the sole party in giving that promise to Abraham. But the Law was a contract between two parties, God, and Israel. Its validity was dependent upon both parties keeping the covenant. (Gal. 3:19b-20)

God kept His covenant with Israel, His part of the bargain, but Israel did not keep its promise to God.

Is the Law then contrary and opposed to the promises of God? Of course not! For if a Law had been given which could give us spiritual life, then righteousness and right standing with God would certainly have come by the Law. But the Scripture pictures all mankind as sinners, shut up and imprisoned by sin, so that the inheritance, the blessing, which was promised through faith in Jesus Christ, the Messiah, might be given, released, delivered, and committed, to all those who believe, who adhere to and trust in and rely on Christ Jesus. Now before the faith came, we were perpetually guarded by and under the Law. We were kept in custody in

> *preparation for the faith that was destined to be revealed, un-
> veiled, disclosed. So that the Law served to us Jews as our trainer,
> our guardian, our guide to Christ to lead us until Christ came,
> that we might be justified, declared righteous, put in right standing
> with God by and through faith. (Gal. 3:21-24)*

Jews have to accept Christ by faith, and the hardest part
of it for us to accept is that our God could come into the world
as a little baby. We were looking for a mighty King, and God
gave us a suffering servant.

> *But now that faith has come, we are no longer under a trainer, the
> guardian of our childhood. For in Christ Jesus you are all sons of
> God through faith. For as many of you as were baptized into Christ
> into a spiritual union and communion with Christ, the Anointed
> One, the Messiah, have put on and clothed yourselves with Christ.
> And now there is no distinction, neither Jew nor Greek, there is
> neither slave nor free, there is not male nor female; for you are all
> one in Christ Jesus. And if you belong to Christ, and you are in
> Him, Who is Abraham's Seed, then you are truly Abraham's
> offspring, and you are spiritual heirs according to the promise.
> (Gal. 3:25-29)*

God gave Abraham four promises: 1) I will bless them
who bless you and curse them who curse you; 2) This land
that you see is yours for everlasting; 3) I will multiply you as
the stars and as the sands of the sea; and 4) through you, all
the nations of the earth shall be blessed. We receive all these
promises that God made to Abraham, because through Christ
Jesus, we become spiritual heirs and sons of Abraham as we
become heirs and co-heirs with Christ Jesus.

Paul, writing to the Ephesians says:

> *And you He made alive, when you were dead, slain by your own
> trespasses and sins in which at one time you walked habitually.
> (Eph. 2:1-2a)*

While we remain in trespass and rebellion, we are dead, because the wages of sin is death. The same message is in the Old Testament and the New. If we count on being saved because of our obedience to the law, we're goners. And we are all in the habit of doing our own thing, which is sin.

> *You were following the course and the fashion of this world. You were under the sway of the tendency of this present age following the prince of the power of the air. You were obedient to him and were under his control, the demon spirit that still constantly works in the sons of disobedience, those who are careless, the rebellious, and the unbelieving who go against the purposes of God. Among these, we as well as you once lived, and we conducted ourselves in the passions of our flesh. Our behavior was governed by our corrupt and sensual nature, obeying the impulses of the flesh and the thoughts of the mind, our cravings dictated by our senses and our dark imaginings. We were then by nature children of God's wrath and heirs of His indignation, like the rest of mankind.*
>
> *But God! Praise God! Because of and in order to satisfy the great and wonderful and intense love with which He loved us, even when we were dead, slain by our own shortcomings and trespasses, He made us alive together in fellowship and in union with Christ Jesus. He gave us the very life of Christ Himself, the same new life with which He quickened Him. For it is by grace, by His favor and mercy which none of us deserve, that we are saved, we are delivered from judgment, and we are made partakers of Christ's salvation. And He raised us up together with Him and He made us sit down together, giving us joint seating with Him, in the heavenly sphere, by virtue of our being in Christ Jesus, the Messiah, the Anoited One. He did this that he might clearly demonstrate through the ages to come the immeasurable, limitless, surpassing riches of His free grace in kindness and goodness of heart toward us in Christ Jesus. For it is by free grace that you are saved, that you are delivered from judgment and you are made partakers of Christ's salvation through your faith. (Eph. 2:2b-8a)*

When Israel gets through the Tribulation and enters into the Millennium, the Lord will give them faith to receive Him. He will pour out His Holy Spirit upon them; He will give

them a new heart, not a heart of stone, but a heart of flesh.
And they will become new creatures in Jesus—by faith.

> *And this salvation is not of yourself or of myself, it is not of your*
> *own doing or of my own doing, it came not through your striving*
> *or my striving, but it is the gift of God. Not because of works . . .*
> *(Eph. 2:8b-9a)*

The fifth prayer a Hebrew must pray every morning (see
page 121 for the first four) is, "Lord, I thank You for giving
me a good deed and a good work that I might do to my fellowman this very day, that it might get into those books up
there to mark off some of the demerits that I've got." If you're
living by works, you've got a book of merits and a book of demerits. Somebody has to keep track. But we are living by
grace. The right to eternal life is not our own doing, it is the
gift of God.

> *Not because of works, not because of the fulfillment of the Law's*
> *demands, lest any man should boast. It is not the result of what any*
> *man could possibly do, so no one can pride himself in it or take*
> *glory to himself. For we are God's own handiwork, His own work-*
> *manship, recreated in Christ Jesus. We are born anew that we may*
> *do those good works which God predestined, planned beforehand,*
> *for us, taking paths which He prepared ahead of time, that we*
> *should walk in them, living the good life which He prearranged*
> *and made ready for us to live. Therefore remember that at one time*
> *you were Gentiles, you were heathen in the flesh; called Uncircum-*
> *cision by those who called themselves Circumcision, itself a mere*
> *mark in the flesh made by human hands. Remember that you were*
> *at that time separated, living apart, from Christ; you were*
> *excluded from all part in Him; you were utterly estranged and out-*
> *lawed from the rights of Israel as a nation, and strangers with no*
> *share in the sacred compacts of the Messianic promise, with no*
> *knowledge of or right in God's agreements, His covenants. And*
> *you had no hope, you had no promise; you were in the world with-*
> *out God.*
> *But praise God, in Christ Jesus, you who once were so far*
> *away, through, by, and in the blood of Christ have been brought*

near. For He is Himself our peace, our bond of unity and harmony. He has made us both Jew and Gentile one body, and He has broken down, destroyed, abolished the hostile dividing wall between us. By abolishing in His own crucified flesh the enmity caused by the Law with its decrees and ordinances, which He annulled, that He from the two might create in Himself one new man, one new quality of humanity out of the two, and therefore, making peace. And He designed to reconcile to God both Jew and Gentile, united in a single body by means of His cross; thereby killing the mutual enmity and bringing the feud to an end. And He came and preached the glad tidings, the good news, the Gospel to you who were afar off and peace to those who were near. For it is through Him that we both, whether we are far off or near, have an introduction, an access, by the same Holy Spirit to the Father so that we are able to approach the Father. (Eph. 2:9-18)

We approach the Father through the Holy Spirit as the Spirit quickens us, and shows us how we can worship in spirit and in truth.

Therefore, you are no longer outsiders, migrants, and aliens excluded from the rights of citizens; but now you share citizenship with the saints, God's own people, which are consecrated and set apart for Himself; and you belong to God's own household. You are built upon the foundation of the apostles and the prophets with Christ Jesus Himself the chief Cornerstone. In Him the whole structure is joined, bound welded together in perfect harmony, and it continues to rise, and to grow, and to increase into a holy temple in the Lord, a sanctuary dedicated, consecrated, and sacred to the presence of the Lord Himself. In Him, and in fellowship with one another, you yourselves also are being built up in this structure with the rest, to form a perfect fixed abode, which is a perfect dwelling place of God in and through Jesus Christ and by the Holy Spirit. (Eph. 2:19-22)

In the period of the Millennium, the Body of believers which have believed in the Lord Jesus Christ and who have been taken up, will be brought back in glorified bodies to be a sanctuary dedicated and sacred to the presence of the Lord.

Chapter 12

Hebrews and Acts

In Hebrews, we find Christ revealed as the better covenant:

Now the main point of what we have to say is this: We have such a High Priest, One Who is seated at the right hand of the majestic God in heaven, as officiating Priest, a Minister in the holy places and in the true tabernacle which is erected not by man but by the Lord. For every high priest is appointed to offer up gifts and sacrifices; so it is essential for this High Priest to have some offering to make also. If then He were still living on earth, He would not be a priest at all, for there are already priests who offer the gifts in accordance with the Law. But these offer service merely as a pattern and as a foreshadowing of what has its true existence and reality in the heavenly sanctuary. For when Moses was about to erect the tabernacle, he was warned by God, saying, See to it that you make it all exactly according to the copy and the model which was shown to you on Mount Sinai. But as it now is, He, Christ, has acquired a priestly ministry which is as much superior and more excellent than the old as the covenant of which He is the Mediator, the Agent, is much superior, more excellent, because it is enacted and rests upon more important–sublimer, higher, and nobler–promises. For if that first covenant had been without defect, there would have been no room for another one or an attempt to institute another one. (Heb. 8:1-7)

163

The defect in the old covenant, which was an expression of God's holiness, was that man cannot live under the expression of His holiness, no matter how hard he tries. There is none good but God. God knew in advance that He would have to come to the earth and go to the cross for you and me because we cannot live in His holiness and fulfill it. He knew He would have to free us by His grace, that He would have to make atonement for us.

> *However, He finds fault with them, showing that it isn't adequate, when He says, Behold, the days will come, says the Lord, when I will make and ratify a new covenant with the house of Israel and with the house of Judah. It will not be like the covenant that I made with their forefathers on the day when I grasped them by the hand to help them, to relieve them, and to lead them up out of the land of Egypt, for they did not abide in My covenant with them, and so I withdrew My favor and disregarded them, says the Lord. For this is the covenant that I will make with the house of Israel after those days, says the Lord. I will imprint My laws upon their minds, even upon their innermost thoughts and understanding. I will take out a hammer and a chisel, and I will engrave them upon their hearts, and I will be their God, and they shall be My people. (Heb. 8:8-10)*

All of this will come to pass in the Millennium, after the Second Coming of Jesus. He will write His laws on our hearts and He will be our God and we will be His people. The covenant of God with Israel is an everlasting covenant.

> *And it will never more be necessary for every one to teach his neighbor and his fellow citizen or every one his brother, saying, Know, perceive, have knowledge of, get acquainted by experience with and get to know the Lord; for all will know Me, from the smallest to the greatest of them. For I will be merciful and gracious toward their sins, and I will remember their deeds of unrighteousness no more. When God speaks of a new covenant, He makes the first one obsolete, out of use. And what is obsolete, out of use, and annulled because of age, is ripe for disappearance and to be dispensed with altogether. (Heb. 8:11-13)*

In the Millennium, Israel will be brought in into the new covenant. The old will pass away because the perfect will be here.

> *Now even the first covenant had its own rules and regulations for divine worship, and it had a sanctuary, but that sanctuary was one of this world. For a tabernacle, a tent, was erected, in the division and the outer compartment of which were the lampstand and the table with its loaves of showbread set forth. This portion is called the Holy Place. (Heb. 9:1-2)*

In the Old Testament sanctuary, twelve loaves of bread were placed on the table every Friday afternoon before sunset, representing each of the tribes of Israel, saying, "Lord, give us this day our daily bread." The loaves would stay there until the following Friday. It was a miracle that the bread was just as fresh on the second Friday as it was when it was placed on the table. It never got moldy, it never got stale. When Christ Jesus taught us how to pray, He said we should ask for our daily bread every day.

> *But inside, beyond the second curtain and the veil, there stood another tabernacle known as the Holy of Holies. In the Holy of Holies, was the golden altar of incense and the ark of the covenant, covered over with wrought gold. This ark contained a golden jar which held the manna. (Heb. 9:3-4a)*

In the wilderness, when the people of Israel kept manna for more than one day, it rotted and bred worms. But the Lord commanded Moses to take a jar of manna, to be as a living witness and testimony for Him, that all Israel would know that He gave them the bread of heaven. And that manna never spoiled. Jesus said, "Your fathers ate of the manna in the wilderness and died, but he who eats of Me, the bread of life, shall never die."

In the wilderness, on the sixth day, God let them gather twice as much manna as usual so they'd have some left over

for the sabbath. That manna didn't spoil. It was as if God said,
"I'll give you twice as much so on the following day you can
worship Me and rest from your labor. You are not to go out
on the sabbath day and generate that mighty dollar that you
worship. I will supply what you need if you give to Me the day
that belongs to Me. On it, you should worship, praise, thank,
and bless Me."

> *The ark of the covenant also held the rod of Aaron which sprouted*
> *and budded, and it held the two tables of stone of the covenant,*
> *bearing the Ten Commandments. (Heb. 9:4b)*

The original two tables of stone which God had made
and on which He had written the ten commandments with
His own finger were broken by Moses when he came down
from his meeting with God on Mount Sinai and found the
people worshiping the golden calf. But Moses made two more
tables of stone, and as God told him the ten commandments
again, he wrote them down.

> *Above the ark and overshadowing the mercy seat were the represen-*
> *tations of the cherubim, the winged creatures which were the sym-*
> *bols of glory. We cannot now go into detail about these things.*
> *(Heb. 9:5)*

Originally, one of the cherubim was Lucifer, Satan. The
other cherubim whose images stood astride the mercy seat of
the ark of the covenant were Michael and Gabriel.

> *These arrangements having thus been made, the priests enter*
> *habitually into the outer division of the tabernacle, in performance*
> *of their ritual acts of worship. But into the second division of the*
> *tabernacle, which is the Holy of Holies, none but the high priest*
> *goes, and he goes in only once a year, and he never goes in without*
> *taking a sacrifice of blood with him, which he offers up for himself*
> *and for the errors and the sins of ignorance and thoughtlessness*
> *which the people of Israel have committed. By this the Holy Spirit*
> *points out that the way into the true Holy of Holies is not yet*

thrown open as long as the former, outer portion of the tabernacle remains a recognized institution and is still standing, seeing that the first, outer portion of the tabernacle was a parable, an allegory, a picture, a visible symbol or a type or a picture of the present age. In it, gifts and sacrifices are offered, and they are yet incapable of perfecting the conscience or of cleansing and renewing the inner man of the worshiper. For the ceremonies deal only with the clean and unclean meats and drinks and different washings, mere external rules and regulations for the body imposed to tide the worshipers over until the time of setting things straight, of reformation, of the complete new order when Christ, the Messiah, shall establish the reality of what these things foreshadow, a better covenant.

But that appointed time came when Christ, the Messiah, appeared as a High Priest of the better things that have come and are still to come. Then, through the greater and more perfect tabernacle, which is not made with human hands, that is, not a part of this material creation, He, Jesus, went once and for all into the Holy of Holies of heaven, not by virtue of the blood of goats and calves by which to make reconciliation between God and man, but by His own blood, having found and secured a complete redemption, an everlasting release for you and me. For if the mere sprinkling of unholy and defiled persons with blood of goats and bulls and with the ashes of a burnt heifer is sufficient for the purification of the body, how much more surely shall the blood of Christ, Who by virtue of His eternal Spirit, His own preexistent divine personality, has offered Himself an unblemished sacrifice to God, to purify our consciences from dead works and lifeless observances to serve the ever-living God?

Christ, the Messiah, is therefore the Negotiator and Mediator of an entirely new covenant, new agreement, so that those who are called and offered it, may receive the fulfillment of the promised everlasting inheritance, since a death has taken place which rescues and delivers and redeems them from the transgressions committed under the old covenant, the first agreement. (Heb. 9:6-15)

A death has taken place, the death of Jesus on the cross, and if we accept and receive Him, we receive the fulfillment of the promise. We have an everlasting inheritance, since Jesus' death rescues and delivers and redeems us from all our transgressions committed under the old covenant. When we receive Jesus as the Messiah, we die with Him and are born again into a new life. As spiritual Israel, we will be taken up in the Body of believers. And in the Millennium, the physical Israel will be delivered.

In the Book of Acts, we see the promise of the coming of the new covenant, when God's people can enter into the rest of God in the period of the Millennium. We can enter into His promised rest the easy way today as the Holy Spirit calls us, draws us, causes us to step out of our seat at an altar call and to say, "Yes, Lord Jesus, I do repent. Yes, Jesus Lord, I do ask You to forgive me of my sins. I know I am a sinner, and I want to enter in with You. I want to be an heir with You. I want to rule with You. So I ask You to forgive me. I open the door of my heart and ask You to save me and heal me in every area of my life.

"Lord, I want to know You personally so that I may spend the Millennium with You as one of your saints and have everlasting life. And Lord, I know that eternal life is not a reward for anything I have done, but it is Your free—and unwarranted—gift. I thank You for the prize, the joy, the cross which was set before You from the beginning of time, from the very foundations of the earth. Jesus, You went to the cross for me, and I do believe and I do profess, and I know I am saved and my house. I know this, I claim it, I believe it, and I stand upon it.

"I will praise You for this from this day forward. I will be still and know that You are God. I will stand still and see Your salvation, because You are the only salvation there is. There's no other. You are the Holy One of Israel. You are the One who sanctified us, justified us, and made us whole. It was You, Lord Jesus, who took upon Yourself the suffering, the anguish, the chastisement that was necessary for me, because all I deserve is the cross, but You went to the cross for me. You even went to hell for me that I might enter into Your kingdom and have everlasting life."

The entire new covenant is based upon the promise of Jesus Christ that He would give us a new heart, forgiveness of ours sins, and the Baptism in the Holy Spirit.

How do we enter into God's promise?

> *Repent, change your mind, change your purpose; turn around and return to God, that your sins may be erased, blotted out, wiped clean, that the times of refreshing, of recovering from the effects of heat–which is sin–that the time of reviving with fresh air–God's Holy Spirit–may come from the presence of the Holy Lord. And that He may send to you, to your heart, the Christ, the Messiah, Who before the foundations of the earth was designated and appointed for you and for me, Jesus our Savior, Whom heaven must receive and retain until the time for the complete restoration of all that God spoke by the mouth of all His holy prophets for all of the ages past, from the most ancient time in the memory of man.*
>
> *Thus said Moses to your forefathers, the Lord God will raise up for you a Prophet from among your brethren as He raised up me; Him you shall listen to and understand by hearing and heed in all things whatever He tells you. And it shall be that every soul that does not listen to and understand by hearing and heed that Prophet shall be utterly exterminated from among the people. (Acts 3:19-23)*

In Old Testament days, Moses knew that there would be only one way for Israel to inherit eternal life, and that would be by way of the Messiah. He saw that anybody who did not listen to Him would be wiped out.

> *Indeed, all the prophets from Samuel and those who came afterward, as many as have spoken, also promised and foretold and proclaimed these coming days. You are the descendants, the sons, of the prophets, and the heirs of the covenant which God made and gave to your forefathers, saying to Abraham, And in your Seed–singular–and in your Heir shall all the families of the earth be blessed and benefited. It was to you first that God sent His Servant and His Son Jesus Christ, when He raised Him up and provided and gave Him to you to bless you in turning everyone of you from your wickedness and your evil ways. (Acts 3:24-26)*

Jesus came into the world that we might go into that
seven-year feast with Him. His banner over us is love, and we
will be with Him during the Millennium and through all eternity.

Look at the prayer of Jesus Christ Himself that we might
enter in and be an heir with Him:

> *When Jesus had spoken these things, He lifted up His eyes to
> heaven and said, Father, the hour is come. Glorify and exalt and
> honor and magnify Your Son, so that Your Son may glorify and
> extol and honor and magnify You. Just as You have granted Him
> power and authority over all flesh, over all human kind, now
> glorify Him, so that He may give eternal life to all whom You have
> given Him. And this is eternal life: it means to know, to perceive,
> to recognize, to become acquainted with and to understand You,
> Father, the only true and real God, and likewise to know Him,
> Jesus, as the Christ, the Anointed One, the Messiah, Whom You
> have sent. I have glorified You down here on the earth by complet-
> ing the work that You gave Me to do. And now, Father, glorify Me
> along with Yourself and restore Me to such majesty and honor in
> Your presence as I had with You before the very world existed.*
>
> *I have manifested Your name, I have revealed Your very
> Self, Your real Self, to the people whom You have given Me out of
> the world. They were Yours, and now Father, You gave them to
> Me, and they have obeyed and kept Your Word. Now, at last, they
> know and understand that all You have given Me belongs to You;
> it is really and truly Yours. For the uttered words that You gave
> Me, I have given them. And they have received and accepted them,
> and they have come to know positively and in reality–to believe
> with absolute assurance–that I came forth from Your presence.
> And they have believed and are convinced that You did send Me. I
> am praying for them. I am not praying and requesting for the
> world; but for those You have given Me, for they belong to You.
> All Mine are Yours, and all that are Yours belong to Me; and I
> am glorified in and through them. They have done Me honor, and
> in them My glory is achieved. And now I am no more in the world,
> but these are in the world, and I am coming to You, Holy Father.
> And Holy Father, keep in Your name, in knowledge of Yourself,
> them whom You have given Me, that they may be one, as We are
> one. While I was with them, I kept and preserved them in Your*

> *name in the knowledge and the worship of You. Those You have*
> *given Me, I have guarded, I have protected, and not one of them*
> *has perished or is lost except the son of perdition, Judas Iscariot,*
> *the one who is now doomed to destruction, destined to be lost that*
> *the Scripture might be fulfilled. (John 17:1-12)*

Jesus, even at the very last moment, held out salvation to
Judas Iscariot. When he refused it, Jesus told him, "Go, and
do what you must do."

For thousands of years, we have blamed the Jews, we
have blamed the Catholics, we have blamed the Roman
soldiers—we have blamed everybody but ourselves for nailing
Jesus to the cross. But He could have called ten thousand le-
gions of angels to rescue Him. He did not, because He was
giving His very own life, laying it down in behalf of His sheep,
and the Father loved Him for doing it.

> *I am the Good Shepherd and I know and recognize My own, and*
> *My own know and recognize Me. Even as truly as the Father*
> *knows Me I also know the Father; and I am giving My very own*
> *life and laying it down in behalf of the sheep. And I have other*
> *sheep besides these, that are not of this fold. I must bring and impel*
> *those also, and they will listen to My voice and heed My call, so*
> *that there will be, they will become, one flock under one Shepherd.*
> *For this the Father loves Me, because I lay down My own life to*
> *take it back again. No one takes it away from Me. On the contrary,*
> *I lay it down voluntarily–I put it from Myself. I am authorized*
> *and have power to lay it down, to resign it; and I am authorized*
> *and have power to take it back again. These are the instructions I*
> *have received as My charge from My father. (John 10:14-18)*

> *And now, Father, I am coming to You. I say these things while I*
> *am still in the world, so that My joy may be made full and com-*
> *plete, and that My joy may be perfect in them; that they may experi-*
> *ence My delight fulfilled in them, that My enjoyment may be per-*
> *fected in their own souls, that they may have My gladness within*
> *them, filling their hearts.*

I have given and delivered unto them Your Word, Your message; and the world has hated them, because they are not of the world, they do not belong to the world; just as I am not of the world. I do not ask that You will take them out of the world, but that You will keep and protect them from the evil one. They are not of the world, they are not worldly, belonging to the world, just as I am not of the world. Therefore, Father, sanctify them, purify them, consecrate them, separate them for Yourself, make them holy by the Truth. Your Word is Truth.

Just as You have sent Me into the world, I also have sent them into the world. And so for their sake and on their behalf I sanctify, dedicate, and consecrate Myself, that they also may be sanctified, dedicated, consecrated, and made holy in the Truth, which is Myself, Christ Jesus.

Neither for these alone do I pray, Father, for it is not for their sake only that I make this request, but also for all those who will ever come to believe in, to cling to, to rely on Me through their word and teaching. So that they all may be one just as You, Father, are in Me and I in You, that they also may be in Us, so that the world may believe and be convinced that You have sent Me. I have given to them the glory and the honor which You have given Me, that they may be one, even as We are one: I in them and You in Me, in order that they may become one and perfectly united, that the world may know and definitely recognize that You sent Me, and that You have loved them even as You have loved Me.

Father, I desire that they also whom You have entrusted to Me, Your gift to Me, may be with Me where I am, so that they may see My glory, which You have given Me, Your love gift to Me, for You loved Me before the foundation of the world. O just and righteous Father, although the world has not known You and has failed to recognize You and has never acknowledged You, I have known You continually. And these men and women understand and know that You have sent Me. I made Your name known to them, and I revealed Your character and Your very Self. (John 17:13-26a)

Jesus revealed the character of God the Father, and He wants us to possess the same character as we reign with Him in the Millennium and in everlasting life. The character of God formed in us is the fruit of the Spirit: love, joy, peace, patience, kindness, goodness, faithfulness, gentleness, and self-control.

And I will continue to make You known, that the love which You have bestowed upon Me may be in them, felt in their hearts, and that I Myself may be in them. (John 17:26b)

This prayer, the Lord's Prayer in John 17, is already answered for those of us who are indwelt by His Holy Spirit. It will be answered for Israel during the Millennium.

No one took Jesus to the cross. He went willingly for the joy that was set before Him of giving us salvation. He willingly bore the pain of it, the humiliation, and the agony.

His was a horrible, agonizing death by torture and asphyxiation, and He died voluntarily, so that He could take His life back up again. And, as He rose from the dead, we rise from the dead with Him into everlasting life. We join Him at the throne of grace, and reign with the King of kings, the Lord of lords next to God the Father, because He is in us and we are in Him.

In the end times, we will see certain people raptured, others able to make it through the Tribulation, and a remnant of Israel saved. We will see the deliverance of Egypt during the Millennium as they turn to Jesus the Savior. The righteous will inherit life, but the apostates will be destroyed. We will see the kingdom united, and then the glorious restoration of Israel.

Could this be the year when the Lord will lift the veil from the eyes of Israel, unstop their ears, and unharden their hearts to believe that Jesus is the Messiah of Israel, the Savior of the world? Is this the turning point of time when every knee shall bow, every tongue confess, that Jesus Christ is Lord?

We do not know. But it could be. Be ready. The King is coming! The next Visitor to planet earth!

———————